Using

visualization

to better

your strokes,

refine your

strategy,

and lower

your score

SIMON & SCHUSTER

New York London Toronto Sydney Tokyo Singapore

VISUAL GOLF

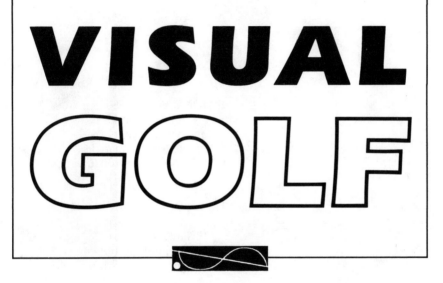

Kenneth Van Kampen

Foreword by
Curtis Strange

Illustrations by
Ken Lewis

SIMON & SCHUSTER
Simon & Schuster Building
Rockefeller Center
1230 Avenue of the Americas
New York, New York 10020

Designed by Carla Weise/Levavi & Levavi
Manufactured in the United States of America

1   3   5   7   9   10   8   6   4   2

Library of Congress Cataloging in Publication Data
Van Kampen, Kenneth.
Visual golf / Kenneth Van Kampen; foreword by Curtis Strange;
illustrations by Ken Lewis.
p.   cm.
1. Golf—Psychological aspects.   2. Imagery (Psychology).
3. Visualization.   I. Title.
GV979.P75V36   1992
796.352'01'9—dc20   91-43936
CIP
ISBN: 0-671-73730-9

Contents

PART III: AROUND THE GREEN

PART IV: PUTTING

PART V: TROUBLE PLAY

Foreword

To play your best golf, you've got to use your head as much as anything else to maneuver the ball around the golf course in as few strokes as possible. Each shot is a new challenge, and to play every one as well as possible, I can't emphasize enough the importance of fully visualizing a golf shot before playing it. "Seeing" the shot happen in your mind is like rehearsing or practicing it before you actually play it. Visualizing a good shot lets you concentrate on all the positive aspects: a smooth swing, solid contact and a good result. It also bolsters your confidence and helps you focus on executing, not on thoughts that could distract you.

Of course, first you've got to know the proper technique for swinging a golf club. If you give a 5-iron to someone who's never hit a ball before and tell him to visualize a good shot and then hit it, he's probably not going to be able to do it because his mind and body don't know how. It's every serious golfer's responsibility to learn the fundamentals of setting up and swinging the golf club if he or she wants to strike a golf ball well. Then visualization can help you learn and improve your swing—just picture what good players look like when they swing and you'll be helping yourself to ingrain those same good habits in your own motion. Once you've learned proper technique, visualization will help you apply it as fully as possible to striking the ball.

I've always considered my ability to plan and imagine the shot clearly before playing it to be one of the strongest aspects of my game. I know that the better I can do that, the better my chances of pulling off each individual shot, and the more likely I'll be to avoid any mental mistakes that could occur throughout the round.

Visualizing the shot will help you to focus on the situation at hand so you can put your best swing on the ball. Here's one example: One of the most important shots I ever had to play was on the 72nd hole of the 1988 U.S. Open. My playing partner, Nick Faldo, and I were tied for the lead when we reached the final tee. The Open was held that year at The Country Club in Brookline, Massachusetts, where the 18th is a long par four measuring 452 yards. Nick drove in the fairway, while I pushed my tee shot into the right rough. He played his approach first and landed it safely on, about 25 feet from the pin, while I followed with a 7-iron that fell short into a bunker in front of the green. With Nick's ball on in regulation, within reasonably easy two-putt range, the ball was now definitely in my court. I can't say that the shot I faced was particularly tough for a tour pro—the lie was clean and slightly uphill, the lip wasn't particularly high, and the pin was only about 30 feet away. (Then again, when the U.S. Open title is on the line, no shot is very easy.) As I stepped into the bunker I reflected on the countless explosion shots I'd practiced, remembering how it felt to pick up the clubhead quickly with my hands, the feeling of the flange bouncing through the sand, the sight of the ball arching gently over the lip and landing close to my target. Then I swung, and the shot happened as I'd pictured it, the ball flopping down on the green and stopping less than two feet from the hole. What a great feeling that was, to see it actually finish where I had pictured it finishing. Nick made a good try with his birdie putt, but it just slid by. He tapped in for his par, then I rolled in my short putt for mine, and we went on to an eighteen-hole playoff the next day, which I won, 71 to 75.

That's just one example of how visualization helped me pull off an important shot, but the truth is, I visualize *every* shot, whether it's a drive, approach, chip or putt. Even when I step up to tap a twelve-inch putt into the cup, I make sure to run the image of the ball dropping into the cup through my head. That's because I always want to maintain a positive feeling from the first tee to the eighteenth green, so as part of my pre-shot routine,

I imagine the shot I want to make in my mind; happening exactly as I hope it will.

Being able to visualize well will also help your ability at shotmaking. If you can't get a clear idea in your head of what you want the ball to do, whether it's bend right or left, fly high or low, then how are you going to hit the shot? The more clearly you can envision what you want to do, the better your chances of doing it. As I said earlier, using your mind to plan and imagine the shot is crucial to a golfer at any level. In fact, amateur players can benefit just as much from visualizing their shots as pros—maybe more. From what I've observed in the many pro-ams I've played in, casual players are far too concerned with swing mechanics on the course, instead of simply planning the shot and swinging the club. Touring pros leave the nuts and bolts of the swing to the practice tee and concentrate more on maneuvering the ball around the course in as few strokes as possible. I think that if more amateurs thought less about their swings and more about making the shot happen instead of *how* they were going to make it happen, they'd score better.

Being adept at visualizing will also help you plan better strategies and avoid making mental mistakes, which is the key to turning in consistently good scores. So my advice to amateur golfers is to work on mental mechanics as well as swing mechanics—you've got to be good at both in order to fulfill your true potential as a player.

Curtis Strange
April 1991

USING YOUR HEAD

1

THE MIND: YOUR MOST IMPORTANT WEAPON

There's a popular saying that golf is 90% mental—indeed, it's one of the most common axioms of the sport. Nevertheless, nearly all instructional books are devoted to the physical side of the game—teaching the correct way to swing a club, strike a chip or stroke a putt. But there's more to it than that. You've got to know how to use your head: Your mind is the most powerful weapon you've got because you need it to learn proper playing techniques, plan intelligent strategies and execute shots consistently.

Most golf instruction books also include a paragraph or two that emphasizes the importance of "visualization"—imagining or picturing the shot before playing it. If you are going to use your mind to learn, plan and execute, you've got to be adept at visualizing.

Unfortunately, there usually is no "how-to" supplied. Although instruction manuals assume the reader needs help physically learning how to hit the ball, they all seem to assume that he or she will automatically be adept at visualizing the shot. However, just as some players are naturally great swingers and some are not, some are also naturally good at visualizing, while others are not. This book will help you improve your golf not only through instruction but also by sharpening your ability to use your mind and visualize. You'll learn to use visualization not only to plan better strategies and execute better ball-striking, but also to improve certain mechanical aspects of your swing.

Simply put, visualization is the act of using your mind to create a picture of something. Webster's defines it: ". . . to see or form a mental image . . ."

Visualization is similar to "imagining"—using your mind to create an "image." The ability to imagine/visualize comes naturally to humans, and is not something that has to be learned, yet our levels of ability can vary. No one had to teach you how to daydream, yet every time you do it, you're visualizing. If you were asked to visualize an apple, an image of what you perceive to be an apple will probably immediately pop into your head. If you were then asked to imagine an orange, you'll conjure a different image, that of an orange.

As you may have guessed, memory helps when visualizing. If you have a memory of what an apple looks like, you can base your visual image on that memory. The same is true with a golf shot: If you've had the experience of hitting a long, high, straight drive, you can recall that image and also the physical feelings you experienced as your body swung the club and impact was made when preparing to hit a tee shot. (The importance of remembering the feeling of a good swing will be touched on later in this chapter.)

The difference between imagining and visualizing is that when you imagine, you may have to invent an image completely. For example, imagine that a golf ball–eating monster lurks in the largest water hazard at your home course, waiting to gobble up any ball that sinks to the bottom. To describe what such a mythical beast would look like, you would have to invent the image, since presumably there is nothing in your visual memory bank to draw on for details. On a golf course, you'll also have to use your powers of imagination when forming a mental movie of the shot you are about to hit, since although you may have a memory of a similar situation to base your picture on, no two shots are exactly alike. You'll have to use your imagination to get a complete picture of the exact shot you want to hit. So from here on, when the word "visualization" is used in this book, it means not only remembering a past experience in your mind's eye, but also involves the use of your imagination in order to help create the image of the shot you are planning to hit.

Now let's get back to the apple. Although you were asked to visualize only what an apple looks like, chances are good you also remembered other characteristics associated with the fruit, such as the smell, the taste and the smooth, firm feel of it in your hand—perhaps even the feeling of sinking your teeth into it.

The same principle applies when visualizing a good golf shot. Take a pitch shot, for example. Not only should you see the image of what the shot looks like, but you also must remember the feeling of the grip in your hands, the rhythmic motion of the clubhead, the solid click of the clubface on the ball, the ball arching softly away from you, then landing on the green next to the pin.

Proper visualization will help put you in a positive state of mind to execute the shot at hand. Too often, golfers worry about the possibility of mishitting the ball or hitting an errant shot, and they let their fears interfere with their ability to make a good swing. By concentrating on visualizing a good result, you calm these fears and assure yourself, that yes, you can make the shot happen.

Visualizing the shot will also help your body to remember the physical feeling of what it's like to execute a well-struck pitch. This is what's known as "muscle memory"—your mind's memory or familiarity with the proper movements needed to perform a given task, whether it's swinging a golf club, throwing a ball or walking down a flight of stairs.

The better you are able to visualize, the better you'll be able to activate the memory of what it "feels" like to hit a good golf shot; and the more able you are at getting in touch with those feelings before the shot, the better your chances of making them happen during the actual act of hitting the ball. Your goal is to activate your "muscle memory" so you can remember what it felt like to make the movements needed to make a good golf shot and repeat them.

In a way, visualization helps you to activate your body's ability to go on "automatic pilot." Think of all the things you do in your life without giving specific conscious thought about them: walking, eating, signing your name, driving. For example, take an experienced driver traveling on an expressway with a large curve looming ahead. He doesn't consciously think, "Okay, I've got to grip the wheel firmly and turn the wheel clockwise slightly by lowering my right hand and raising my left hand. I have to turn the wheel about this much to stay on the road . . ." An experienced driver won't have to talk to himself like that; instead, the proper actions needed to steer the car through the curve will happen automatically as his mind reacts to it, so the road seems to straighten out magically in front of his eyes as the bend is negotiated. He doesn't consciously think about turning through the curve, he simply *reacts* to it.

Visualizing the shot before hitting it will help you activate the memory of what it feels like to hit a good shot, increasing your chances of making a good swing.

The same is true when you hit a golf ball—you shouldn't have to think about the specific motions you make when swinging the club, i.e., "Swing back slowly, keeping the left arm straight and head still while shifting the weight onto the inside of the right foot." An experienced player has done enough playing and practicing to know the mechanics of hitting the ball. Instead, he should be able to examine the situation, decide on the kind of shot he'd like to hit, then let his body react to the situation.

Perhaps the greatest example in golf of a player simply reacting to the ball was Ken Venturi's victory in the 1964 U.S. Open at Congressional Country Club. In 1964 and years prior, the final two rounds of the Open were played on one day—the third round on Saturday morning, followed by the fourth in the afternoon. (The format was changed the following year so the fourth round was played on Sunday, and it has remained that way since.) Venturi started the third round six strokes out of the lead, but shot 68 and closed the gap to two. Throughout the morning, however, the heat and humidity had risen dramatically, taking its toll on Venturi, and after finishing he nearly collapsed from exhaustion and dehydration. But his will to finish the tournament was strong, and after drinking several iced teas and taking salt tablets, in less than an hour he was back on the first tee to start the final round. A doctor carrying more salt tablets and a bag of ice walked with him, and by the time Venturi made the turn he had gained the lead, but his condition had worsened. He walked the remaining fairways in a slow, tired daze; he simply arrived at each shot, sized up the situation, planned the shot, then reacted to the ball—he had no energy for any other kind of thought. But the talent and ability were there for him to draw on, and the result was an incoming 35 and a winning margin of four strokes.

REACTING IN OTHER SPORTS

Consider fast-paced sports in which you have to react to the ball. A baseball batter doesn't have time to think about how to swing the bat because the pitch comes in at high speed. He has to see it and react to it. A basketball player doesn't stop and say to himself, "Hmmm, I'm about twenty feet from the hoop, so I have to release the ball with this much force, and I'd better make sure to square my shoulders to the hoop and follow through . . ." Instead, he sees the hoop and reacts to it. A tennis player doesn't have time to think, especially when playing close to the net;

instead, he allows his reflexes and muscle memory to take over.

Of course in golf you don't have to hit a moving ball, which leaves you plenty of time to think between shots and as you stand over the ball at address, readying to pull the trigger. That opportunity to think often proves damaging, since it can allow negative thoughts to crop up, which interfere with the individual's ability to hit a good shot.

THINK LESS, REACT MORE

The ability to visualize well will help your body react to the shot without your having to think about it consciously. An experienced player *knows* how to hit a golf ball. However, he may not be able to trust himself simply to let his body do it without his mind interfering. Yet once you've learned how to do something, you don't need to tell yourself how to do it over and over again. You've probably had the experience of hitting a "no-brainer": For one reason or another you just stepped up to the ball and hit it without giving the swing much thought, and, lo and behold, you hit a great shot. It's amazing what you're capable of doing when you simply react without thinking. Your ultimate goal should be simply to plan the shot, visualize it, then hit it.

Visualization usually happens naturally, to some degree, before performing any target-oriented task. Let's go back to basketball again for an example. If you stand at the foul line readying to shoot a foul shot, the image of the ball falling through the net will come to mind almost automatically. It makes sense, since making the shot is your goal. In the instant it takes a tennis player to react to a shot and plan a hard, deep ground stroke to the other end of the court, the image of the ball bouncing just inside the back line flashes through his mind. A billiards player, lining up a shot, sees the image of the shot successfully executed in his head before he shoots—his own smooth stroke on the cue ball, the cue ball striking the target ball, and the ball rolling toward the pocket and dropping cleanly in. Likewise, a bowler, as he pauses to concentrate before starting his motion, "sees" the ball rolling down the alley, hitting the pocket firmly between the one and three pins and converting a strike.

However, just as you can visualize a positive outcome, you can also envision a *negative* result, which is obviously detrimental to physical performance and will block you from achieving your goal. Negative thoughts most often occur when there is some sort of pressure on you to perform. Suppose you need to make a three-foot putt on the final hole to tie a big match. As you prepare to hit it, all the negative things that will result if you miss it start running through your mind: You've lost the match because you couldn't sink a lousy three-footer when you needed to. You've lost the bet. You've failed. You've "choked." Other people will think you've choked . . . Along with these types of thoughts, you also start imagining all the possible ways of missing the putt: pulling it left, pushing it right, leaving it short, hitting it too hard, lipping it out—all negative visualization. And though you may try to substitute a positive picture of the ball going in the hole, usually the negative "talk" and images that are dominating your mind are too powerful and overwhelm any attempt to be positive.

Unfortunately, there doesn't necessarily even have to be pressure on for negative thoughts to intrude. Perhaps you've had the experience of stepping up to an approach shot and inexplicably getting the feeling that you'll pull the ball left of the green. You aren't sure why, but something makes you think that's what's going to happen. The vision of the ball sailing off course and landing left of the target projects itself clearly in your head. Consequently, you pull the shot left, and the first words out of your mouth are, "I knew I was going to do that!" The fact that you clearly visualized the shot, even though you didn't want to, helped make it happen.

The solution is to improve your mind power so you can create a positive image that will override any negative images or ideas that could occur and disrupt your ability to execute the shot successfully. The more detail you can visualize, the more fully occupied your mind will be, allowing less chance for negative thoughts and images to crop up.

HOW DOES YOUR VISUALIZATION RATE?

How sharp is your present ability to visualize? Most golfers fancy themselves to be pretty good at picturing what a shot will look like, but in fact leave out a lot of relevant details. Following are four visualization "tests." In each, you will be given a sparse description of a situation. Your job is to picture the scene and ensuing shot in your mind as fully as you can. If you wish, you can use a pencil and paper to list the details.

Test Number 1: 150-yard Approach to an Elevated Green

[Take a moment to get a clear, complete picture in your mind, and when you're satisfied with it, answer the following questions. Be honest with yourself if you didn't consider certain details.]

- What was the lie like?
- Where on the green was the pin cut?
- What was the character of the wind?
- What club did you choose?
- Did conditions cause you to choose more club than usual?
- Were there any obstacles—sand, water, trees—to negotiate?
- Did you make a practice swing?

- How did the shot feel?
- Did you hit a draw or a fade?
- Did you take a divot?
- Could you see the ball bounce?

How did you do? Was the picture in your mind detailed enough to allow you to answer most of these questions? If you couldn't answer three or more because you failed to consider them, don't be discouraged, since this was your first test. However, it is an indication that you need to work on conjuring a more complete picture in your head. Try another.

Test Number 2: Tee Shot to a Tight Fairway
- What made the fairway tight—trees, sand, water, rough?
- Was the tee elevated?
- What club did you select?
- How high did you tee the ball?
- What was the wind like?
- Did you hit it solid?
- Did you play a draw or a fade?
- Was the trajectory high or low?
- Did the ball run much after it landed?

Test Number 3: Greenside Sand Explosion
- What kind of lie was it—clean, a "fried egg," or buried?
- Was the sand especially firm or fluffy?
- About how far was the pin from the ball?
- About how much green did you have to work with?
- Did the shot check up quickly after landing?
- Where did the ball finish in relation to the pin?

Test Number 4: 30-foot Putt
- Which way did it break?
- Was it uphill or downhill?
- Did you make a practice stroke?
- Did you make it? If yes, did you topple it over the edge or charge it into the back of the cup?
- If you missed, where did the ball finish?
- What was the speed of the green like?

How did you do? Hopefully, as you progressed from test to test, you realized that the idea was to include as much detail as possible, and so you added more and more each time, giving yourself a more vivid picture of the situation. You can practice further by creating your own imaginary situations.

DIRECTING YOUR MENTAL MOVIE

When it comes to what you see in your head, you are responsible for the image. You should always visualize the entire shot, from start to finish. Remember that there may be certain aspects of the shot that you want to revisualize and concentrate on more heavily as director of the movie, depending on exactly what you are trying to accomplish.

For example, suppose you face a tee shot to a blind landing area, or an approach to a blind green. You'll want to "see" the entire shot from beginning to end. But after that, you'll gain even more confidence by reviewing the beginning of the shot—the ball streaking away on the intended target line. Why focus on the beginning of the shot? Because in this situation, where you can't see the landing area, the most easily accessible image you will be able to form is of the shot starting on the right path.

In other situations, the middle of the ball's flight will be the best part to review after first visualizing the shot. For example, imagine a player facing an approach shot to a green protected by water on the front and right side. The player needs to get on safely, and so decides to aim away from the water and fade the ball into the green, although a draw is his natural shot. To help

When facing a shot to a blind landing area, the part of the shot you should focus on most is the beginning, as the ball streaks away on the intended line.

For certain shots, such as when trying to manufacture a draw or fade, it will help you the most to concentrate on the middle of the ball's flight.

increase the chances of manufacturing a fade, the best part of the shot to key on would be the middle, as the ball peaks and gently curves from left to right.

Finally, there will be certain situations when the very end of a shot—when it lands and comes to a stop—will be best to review after fully visualizing what you want to do. Such a time might be when you've got to hit a pitch close to the hole. Then you should focus hardest on the end of the shot, clearly imagining the ball landing stiff to the pin and holding fast right next to the cup.

The next time you play, carry your visualization a step further by not just visualizing the entire shot, but also by concentrating on a specific part. Since you are the director of your mental movie, which part of the shot you choose to focus more attention on will depend upon what exactly you have to do with the ball. The more you practice, the better you'll get at recognizing which segment—beginning, middle or end—you should emphasize and review in your private picture show.

Sometimes the very end of the shot—when the ball lands and comes to a stop—is the best part to emphasize when visualizing the proposed outcome.

IMPROVING YOUR ABILITY TO VISUALIZE

Once in a while people who love golf will find themselves daydreaming about playing (sometimes it's the only thing that can get an avid player through a long, cold winter). When you fantasize about playing golf, you are visualizing. In fact, you can improve your ability to visualize when you daydream.

The next time you decide to sit back and play a few holes or hit a few shots in your mind, make a conscious effort to inject more details into your mental movie. What are you wearing? Who are you playing with? What kind of ball are you using? What number is on it? What kind of golf glove are you wearing? Although these things don't specifically have anything to do with how you swing the club or hit a certain shot, imagining them will help you to expand and build your visualization power. The more you practice forming a detailed picture in your head, the easier and more automatically it will happen when you are actually out playing. And the more vividly you can visualize the situation you hope to make happen—a successful shot—the better you'll be able to prepare yourself to make the physical moves required to make the situation—the shot—happen.

REWIND AND REPLAY

Another common practice among golfers is, after playing a round, to reflect on the especially good shots they have hit. One of the most enjoyable parts of visiting the "19th hole" with your playing partners is talking about the highlights of the day.

Not only is reliving a good shot a pleasant experience, it is also valuable because it reinforces the memory of a good performance. Keeping that in your memory bank will allow you to call upon it when you face a similar situation.

For example, you're playing a match and bunker your tee shot on a par four. Your opponent, having driven shorter but in the fairway, puts his approach shot on the green. You've got to follow suit out of the hazard. You reflect back to last week, when you faced a similar shot with the same club, and hit a good shot. You recall how you prepared for the shot, how you keyed on making a slow takeaway, three-quarter swing and solid contact. The feeling of solid impact and seeing the ball hanging in the air and dropping on the green floods your mind. Confidence builds —you know you can hit this shot, you've done it before . . . Thus, recalling a past successful experience can help you to pull off another one, even in a tough situation.

PLAY IT TWO WAYS

The next time you practice short pitches and chips, try this exercise. Take two clubs, a pitching wedge and a 5-iron, and hit shots from a variety of different lies. From each lie, hit two shots, one with the wedge, the second with the 5-iron. You'll find that, depending on where the ball lies in relation to the edge of the green and the hole, that one club is probably better suited than the other. When there's little green to work with, the wedge is preferable because you can loft the ball to the target. The 5-iron is the better choice when there's plenty of green between the ball and the hole, since it's better suited to hit a low, running shot, allowing you to roll the ball up close like a putt.

This two-club game allows you to play the shot as you would normally, with the ideal club, while also forcing you to improvise using a less than ideal club to play a less than run-of-the-mill shot. Anytime you have to try anything out of the ordinary, in golf or anything else, you are usually forced to stop and give a little extra thought to planning your maneuver. When you have to change the way you typically play a shot, it forces you to work a little harder at picturing the shot in your mind. The more times you have to do this, the better you will become at picturing and inventing shots.

"ONE-CLUB"

Anyone who's been around golf for a while has probably heard of, if not played, "one-club," a game in which you choose a single club to play the course, using it as your sole weapon to advance the ball from tee to cup. When you play one-club you'll find that you rarely have the exact club you need for the situation at hand (for example, you may find yourself 40 yards from the green with a 4-iron in your hand), forcing you to improvise and "invent" different shots. And, to invent shots, you have to be able to visualize them.

If you've never tried this game, grab a friend or two and play a few holes. You can either allow each player the right to choose whatever club he wishes from this bag, or you can all agree to use the same stick; for example, everyone takes their 7-iron.

Not only will one-club improve your ability to visualize, it will also improve your feel on short shots and your overall shot-making ability. One of the most talented shotmakers of all time, Seve Ballesteros, credits much of his ability to the fact that he learned to play the game with only one club—a 3-iron. Because he was limited to that club, Seve was forced to learn to hit a great number of different shots with it. (He can even explode from greenside sand with his 3-iron—and land the ball with backspin!) Today, he is known for his ability to create imaginative shots to fit any situation, which is why he is also known as one of the best trouble players in the game.

Although playing one-club may not turn you into a Seve Ballesteros, it will improve your visualization and playing abilities. On top of that, it's a lot of fun.

3

WHAT'S A "SHOT"?

What exactly is a shot? When does it start? Most amateurs would say that it begins when the clubface makes contact with the ball. A pro, however, would answer that a shot begins with what's known as a *preshot routine*—the sequence of actions and thoughts that a player makes as he readies himself to hit a shot. The purpose of such a routine is, first, to gather all the information needed to determine where the ball should be hit and the kind of shot needed to get it there; and second, at the same time, to shut out any outside distractions that could disturb the player's thinking process. The best way to make sure that visualization becomes a habit is to make it part of this routine. At professional tournaments, it's obvious that the players don't haphazardly grab a club and hit the ball. Each has a specific set of steps, like a ritual, that he performs to plan the shot and to prepare himself to hit it.

To give you an idea of a typical preshot routine, following is an example of what one player may do to prepare for a shot:

First, he checks the lie of his ball to see if it will limit the kind of shot he can play. Next, he determines where he wants to advance the ball from that point. He takes note of the strength and direction of the wind. Using all the information he's gathered, he chooses the club he'll need. Then he visualizes the shot, perhaps concentrating on a specific part of it, and perhaps making a practice swing to help get the feeling of what the swing

Step 1: Size up the situation and decide the way you want to play the shot.

Step 2: Choose the club and fully visualize the shot planned.

Step 3: Step up to the ball, first aiming the clubface squarely at an intermediate target.

Step 4: Assume address position, aligning your body in relation to the clubface. Waggle for comfort, then swing.

will feel like. Now he's ready to address the ball, so he steps behind it and picks out an intermediate target a few feet in front of the ball. He then steps up to the ball and aims the clubface squarely at the intermediate target, aligning his body according to the leading edge of the clubface. He adjusts his feet slightly until he's comfortable, then waggles the club once to loosen his forearms before starting the takeaway.

This is merely an example of a preshot routine, not a blueprint. Every player's will vary slightly. The important thing is that it allows you to gather all the information you need and to focus on the task at hand. The routine should move quickly: Although the above process may have sounded long and drawn out, it probably took longer to read about it than to perform it.

REPEATING THE ROUTINE HELPS YOU REPEAT THE SWING

A key to playing good golf is being able to repeat the same swing time after time, so it's also important that your preshot routine be consistent. In other words, if you want to repeat the same basic swing each time you step up to the ball, you should repeat your preparation process every time as well. The fact is, although it's called the preshot routine, most tour pros actually think of it as being part of the shot, in that they wouldn't think of hitting a ball in competition without performing it. Whenever you see a tour pro become distracted by something after taking address—a noise or a motion in the gallery, perhaps—he'll always step completely away from the ball and run through his preshot routine again in order to reestablish his focus. Just watch the eyes of players like Jack Nicklaus, Raymond Floyd or Curtis Strange as they get ready to hit a shot and you'll get an idea of how well focused they are on what they are doing. That's the same kind of concentration that every golfer should strive for. Golf is a game of thinking and strategy, and the better you are able to concentrate, the fewer mistakes you'll make, saving you a lot of strokes. Tour pros get more upset with themselves when they make mental mistakes rather than physical mistakes. That's because physical mistakes are bound to happen: No one is a robot, so even pros can't be expected to swing the club perfectly every time. But mental mistakes can, and should, be avoided.

Concentrating on the game can be demanding for an amateur player since a big part of playing casual golf is the camaraderie of being with friends and a certain amount of socializing between shots is bound to take place. That's one of the reasons the game is fun, but it can make it difficult to maintain concentration. A good preshot routine will help you to forget the small talk for a moment and focus in for a few seconds in order to hit a good shot.

MAKE IT A ROUTINE BEFORE EVERY SHOT

Your preshot routine should be performed before every shot, whether it's a drive, approach, pitch, chip or putt. In fact, putting is where it will count most, since that aspect of the game takes the most concentration and requires you to be the most precise. If you are ever disturbed while standing over a putt, odds are good that you'll hit a poor putt unless you step away from it and run through your preshot routine again. A classic example of this came in the 1970 British Open at St. Andrews, Scotland. Playing the final hole of the tournament, Doug Sanders stood poised over a three-foot putt for the win. Suddenly, he bent down to brush away a small impediment on the line, but rather than stepping away from the ball and readying himself again, he instead resumed his address position, stroked and missed. Legend has it that Ben Hogan, watching the tournament on television back in the United States, shouted for him to step away from the putt. The miss dropped Sanders into a tie with Jack Nicklaus, who won the playoff by a single shot the following day. Who knows what would have happened had Sanders stepped away and recomposed himself?

Hopefully, you won't have to wonder about the fate of one of your own shots if you perform your routine each time you hit the ball and repeat it if for some reason you are distracted after you take address. It will be worth the extra few seconds.

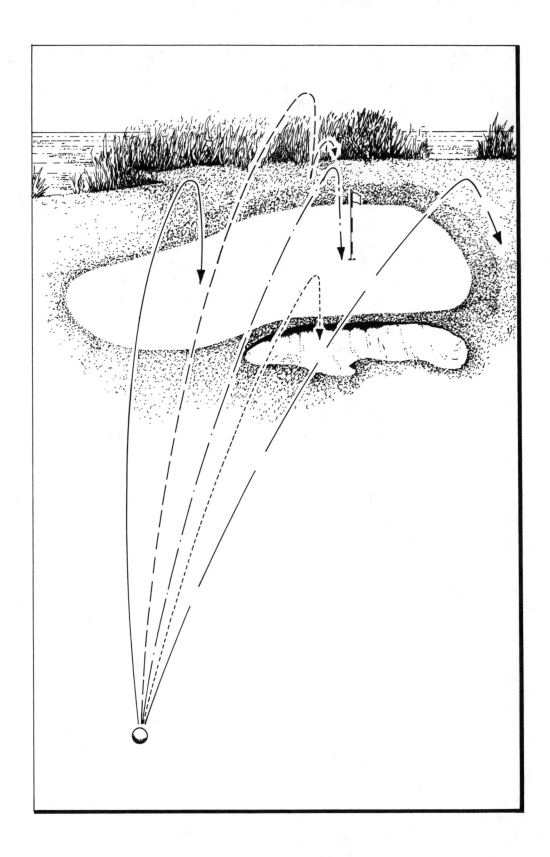

SETTING, SEEING AND REACHING YOUR GOALS

After the third round of the 1960 U.S. Open at Cherry Hills Golf Club in Denver, Colorado, Arnold Palmer trailed the leader, Mike Souchak, by seven shots. Before teeing off for the final eighteen, Palmer confronted a few sportswriters in the locker room and playfully asked them if they thought a 65 would steal the title. "Sure," one writer laughed, "if Ben Hogan shoots it." Arnold laughed too, but he wasn't joking.

The first hole at Cherry Hills is a short par four, at that time measuring 346 yards, though playing even shorter in the thin mountain air, so that the green was drivable for a big hitter. Though the hole lacked a great deal of length, it made up for it by being narrow. A jagged line of poplars and pines closely bordered the left side of the fairway, and a large ditch on the right guarded the landing area. In the opening round Palmer had found the ditch with his drive, took a drop and eventually made double-bogey six. He abandoned efforts to drive the green in the next two rounds, but with a target score of 65 he needed to get out of the blocks fast, so he decided to go for it again. The ball was struck clean, hard and this time straight; it bounced in the fairway, skidded through a bar of heavy rough fronting the green (meant to snare long hitters) and rolled onto the putting surface, stopping 20 feet from the flag. From there he two-putted for birdie, the first of seven en route to a 65—and a one-shot victory.

The moral of the story is that Palmer didn't just happen to go out and shoot 65. He had it in mind from the start; it was his goal. He didn't drive the green by accident, it was his intention. In contrast, most amateurs are vague about their goals. Most will admit to wanting to "play well," to hoping to "turn in a good score." It helps to be more specific, to plan your attack on the course beforehand. Determine which holes play to your strengths and thus offer the best scoring opportunities, and which holes will be the most difficult challenges. You can always change your strategy as you go if need be, but the important thing is to think it through *before* you begin play.

As emphasized earlier, part of the reason behind visualizing a shot before playing it is to help get familiar with the physical action it will take to produce that shot—in a way rehearsing it before playing it. Formulating a goal and a game plan before a round will help accomplish the same thing. Gary Player underscored this idea in his book *Golf Begins at 50* when he wrote:

> . . . you've got to "see" your goals happening in your mind's eye for them to become a fact . . . [Before] the 1987 U.S. Senior Open . . . I did a lot of visualization . . . In practice rounds I visualized every shot that I would have to play. That's why I stuck to my plan of hitting 1-irons off the tees where I had to have great accuracy . . . On the final practice day, I went out onto the eighteenth green, and nobody was there. I saw myself playing the last hole, [telling myself] you might need a four to win, and this is what you'll have to do, this is the shot you'll have to hit, and I ended up seeing myself getting the trophy. For a moment there, the visualization became quite real to me: I was standing there receiving the trophy . . . I'm telling you these things because I think it shows the extent to which you can take this visualizing of your goals. Of course, you won't win every match just because you visualize winning. However, I'll say this: You have a far better chance of success if you do it, and do it strongly, than if you have fuzzy goals and don't work at them.*

Having a clear idea of what you hope to accomplish and how you are going to go about making it happen will help you quiet your mind before the start of the round. Even if you've never played the course, see if you can find out something about its characteristics beforehand: Is it tight? Is it long? Are the greens

* Gary Player with Desmond Tolhurst, *Golf Begins at 50*, (New York: Simon & Schuster, 1988), p. 234–5.

very fast or undulating? Getting your mental juices flowing in advance will put you in the right frame of mind to achieve your goals. You'll have the feeling that you've readied yourself mentally and that you aren't simply blundering to the first tee unprepared.

Any golfer who's ever had to sleep on a third-round lead will tell you that on the night before the final round, one of the things they do is to imagine how they are going to play the final round to hold the lead and claim victory. Will it be better to play defensively and turn in a score around par? Or does the course lend itself to low scores, presenting the possibility that someone could get hot, take the lead, and eventually win? If so, the strategy should be to play aggressively and add to the lead. What target score should result in victory? Which holes have posed problems so far, and should strategy be changed to negotiate them better? If a change in strategy is in order, the player will be sure to visualize the new game plan in detail from tee to green.

Being able to plan effective strategies according to your personal abilities is extremely important in determining whether you reach your scoring potential. The key to planning effective scoring strategies is to carefully weigh the risks involved on every shot and determine whether taking a gamble is truly worth it. Golf is full of gambles, some greater than others. If a gamble doesn't pay off, the penalty is usually putting your ball into some form of trouble, such as rough, sand, water, woods, or uneven lies. Getting into a trouble situation can inflate your score because it will usually be difficult and sometimes impossible to play out of. Most golfers know that if they miss a green with an approach and instead put the ball in a bunker, they will have to work hard to save par, and that the odds are high that they'll make bogey (or worse) instead. And some forms of trouble result in automatic penalty strokes: hitting a shot out of bounds, taking an unplayable lie, losing a ball, hitting a ball into a position in a hazard where you can't play it out.

The more you can avoid putting yourself in these types of situations, the better you should score. That's why you should always aim for the point in the fairway that will allow you the combination of the best lie and the best angle to the pin. Of course, no golfer is perfect, and not every shot goes where planned, so during the course of any round you're going to have to flirt with hazards. How much you flirt is up to you. For example, if a pin is cut close to the right side of the green, next to a bunker, you may want to aim away from it toward the center of the green, rather than trying to stick the shot close and risk finding the trap.

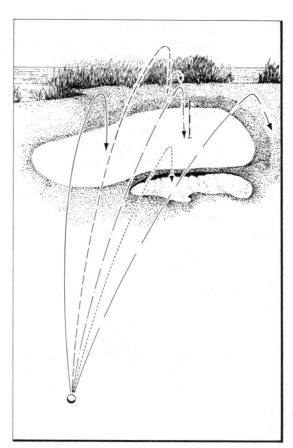

In order to plan the best strategy, carefully weigh all the risks involved with each shot and picture all the possibilities.

Under certain circumstances, it may be best to aim where you are least likely to get into trouble. In the 1991 Masters, Ian Woosnam and Tom Watson, playing together, reached the final tee in a tie for the lead. The 18th hole at Augusta National is a long, uphill par four that doglegs slightly to the right. Trees guard the right side of the fairway where tee shots land, while two large bunkers flank the left side. Watson chose to fade a 3-wood down the right side, but pushed it into the woods. Woosnam, on the other hand, aimed down the left side of the fairway and blasted it with a driver, knowing that if he hit the ball well he'd carry it past the traps, giving himself a shot to the green whether it landed in the fairway or not. Even if it finished in the sand, he'd still be able to go for the green. Woosnam's strategy worked: He hit it hard and carried the bunkers, and even though it hooked left and finished in the practice area, he still had a clear shot to the green with an 8-iron. Watson had much less to work with and ended up punching a low draw out of the trees that finished in a trap to the front-left of the green. Woosnam hit his approach to the fringe and two-putted for four; Watson blasted out but missed his par putt, and the green jacket went to Woosie.

TAILOR YOUR STRATEGY TO YOUR GAME

The type of strategy you choose will depend upon your abilities. Long hitters will usually plan to try to get home in two on most par fives, while average hitters will try to make birdie by playing for the best possible fairway position and one-putting after reaching the green in three.

The strategy you decide upon should play to your strengths and away from risks. It sounds like common sense, but oftentimes amateurs aren't creative enough when planning their strategies because they are afraid they won't be playing the way the originators of the game intended. In theory, on a par-three hole you are regulated one shot to hit the green, then two putts, equaling three. On a par four, you are regulated two shots to get the ball on the green, then two putts, and on a par five, you are regulated three shots to put the ball on the green with two putts.

Because of that, nearly all golfers believe that to play the game properly they have to go for the green in regulation. But that's not always wise. A case in point is the golfer who finds himself in the fairway of a long par four with a three-wood approach to a well-bunkered green. The chances of getting the ball safely on are minimal at best, while the chances of landing in trouble are high. Faced with this situation, most amateurs will still go for the green because they have it in their heads that they have to hit every green in regulation. One of the beauties of golf, however, is that it doesn't matter how you make your score on a given hole—the only thing that shows up on the scorecard is the number of strokes you took. So whether you hit the green of a particular par five in regulation with your third shot and take two putts for par, or come up short of the green in four shots and hole a chip for par, the bottom line is that both players made the same score: Five. So it really doesn't matter how you arrive at the number, as long as you get there.

With that in mind, the percentage play for the player mentioned above would then be to hit less club and lay up short of the green to an area that will allow him a good chance to pitch close and one-putt for par. If the odds are great that you'll miss the green, you might as well land in an area that will give you the best chance of getting up and down for the four. Ben Hogan practiced a similar strategy on the 11th hole at Augusta National, a par four requiring a medium-iron approach to a green guarded closely by a pond on the front and left. Instead of going for the green with his second shot, Hogan would intentionally play to the right of it, away from the water, no matter how well he had driven the ball. The reason was that he felt the risk of putting the approach in the water was too great, so he would rather play safely away from it into an area that would allow him a good chance to chip close and one-putt for par. Hogan won the tournament twice using this strategy on number 11, once saying that if you ever saw him on that green in two, you'd know he mishit his second shot.

Because there is certainly more than one way to play a particular golf hole, you have to figure out the best way for you. For example, Palmer had the length with his driver to reach the green on the 1st hole at Cherry Hills. Most players don't have that kind of power, so it wouldn't make sense for them to risk hitting a driver—the smarter play would be to hit less club, like a three-wood, in an attempt to keep the shot under control and land it safely in the narrow fairway. In other words, it probably won't be worth the risk to use driver on a short, tight hole if you can't hit the green, since teeing off with less club will still leave you with a short-iron approach shot.

Take a moment to think about your home course. Is there one or more hole in particular that's your "nemesis," that you always seem to make double bogey on when you play it? If so, give some thought to changing your strategy.

THE BETTER YOU PLAN, THE FEWER MISTAKES YOU MAKE

Your goal should be to eliminate the words "should have" from your golf vocabulary. Doing that involves thinking carefully before the shot and considering all the possibilities when you visualize the shot you want to play. The better you plan your strategy, the fewer mental mistakes you'll make. Remember that physical errors are going to happen—you're occasionally going to put a bad swing on the ball because you aren't a machine. But mental errors can, and should, be avoided.

PART II

THE
SWING

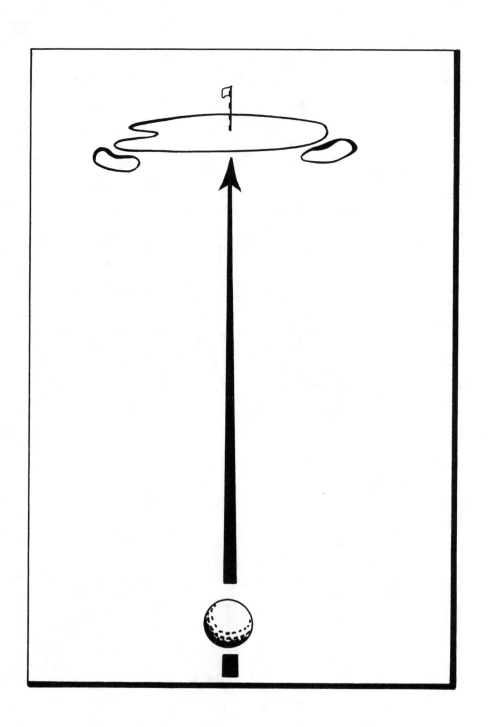

PRESWING BASICS

Visualization will help you fully and successfully use your physical techniques to hit a good shot. But if your technique is poor, even good visualization won't help, so you do have to devote some time to the nuts and bolts of the swing in order to hit the ball well.

In order to make a good golf swing, first you have to put your body in the most favorable position to make all the correct moves. There are certain basics that every golfer must adhere to in order to get into the proper "ready" position before swinging, known as the *address*. To assume a good address, you need to pay close attention to certain preswing basics—grip, posture and alignment. Don't ever underestimate the importance of developing and maintaining solid preswing basics. Trying to make a decent swing without first establishing the basics is like trying to build a house on a poor foundation.

HOW TO TAKE A GOOD GRIP

The way you hold the club is crucial to good ball-striking. A proper grip allows you to release the club correctly and powerfully through the ball while maintaining a firm hold from the start of the swing to the finish. A faulty grip, on the other hand, will force you to make compensations to get the clubface squarely on the ball.

To hold the club correctly to make a right-handed swing (all swing instruction will be worded for players swinging from the right side; golfers who swing from the left side should substitute the words "left" for "right" and "right" for "left" to make the swing instruction applicable to themselves), lay the handle across your left palm and close your hand, wedging the butt end of the grip against the heel pad with the last three fingers. Lay the thumb on the shaft, just right of center. Make sure there are no gaps between any of your fingers and that you have a secure, but not tight, hold.

Now take hold with our right hand, cradling the handle in the crooks of your fingers and laying your thumb on the grip just left of center. You can unite your hands by forming the *interlocking grip* (right little finger interweaved with the left index finger) or the *overlapping grip* (laying the right little finger atop the valley formed between the index and middle fingers on the left hand). Or, you can simply butt the left index finger against the right little finger to form the *ten-finger grip*.

One more thing you have to check is *grip position:* If your hands are turned too far to the left or right, you'll have trouble squaring the clubface to the ball at impact, resulting in crooked shots. To check your position, first note that the valley formed by the fleshy fold between each thumb and hand forms a V shape. Where those Vs point will determine your grip position.

The interlocking grip.

The overlapping grip.

The ten-finger grip.

A neutral grip position is achieved when the Vs formed by the thumb and index fingers of both hands point directly over your right shoulder.

Good position will find the Vs pointing anywhere between your nose and the outer edge of your right shoulder. If the Vs point anywhere between those boundaries, you're okay.

You'll have to experiment with your grip position to find out exactly where the Vs should point in order for you to square the clubface to the ball at impact. The average player will usually be most successful with a *neutral* grip position, so the Vs point approximately midway between the nose and right shoulder, about at the right armpit.

Stronger players with active hands usually prefer to point the Vs more toward their nose, in what's termed a *weak* position, since they make a powerful release and have little trouble squaring the clubface at impact. But if the Vs point left of your nose, your grip is too weak and you'll have difficulty squaring the club to the ball on the downswing. Instead, you'll most likely leave the clubface open at impact, causing the shot to go right. Trying to play with a very weak grip typically causes what's known as *casting*, a timing problem in which the golfer attempts to square the clubface by releasing the club too hard, disrupting the critical synchronization between the upper and lower body and resulting in an inside-out downswing path.

Golfers with less physical strength, such as children, ladies and seniors, should favor a *strong* grip position, so the Vs point more toward the right shoulder. This position makes it easier to square the clubface to the ball at impact and promotes drawspin, which will make the ball go farther.

Be aware, though, that if the Vs point to the right of your shoulder, your position is too strong, which will lead to closing the clubface before it reaches the ball on the downswing, causing the shot to go left. Often, playing with an overly strong grip will lead to *blocking,* or inhibiting the release of the hands on the downswing in order to keep the face from closing before impact at the sacrifice of clubhead speed.

PERFECT POSTURE

The way you stand up to the ball sets up the kind of swing you make. Good posture puts you in the proper position to swing on the proper plane, make a good body turn and maintain complete balance, all of which contributes to returning the clubface squarely and powerfully to the ball on the downswing.

The first step toward good posture is to make sure your feet are the proper distance apart. If your stance is too wide, it will restrict the proper leg action and hip turn. On the other hand, if your feet are too close together, you'll have balance problems, causing your upper body to sway to the right on the backswing. Ideally, your feet should be about as far apart as your shoulders are wide, or just slightly wider. Stance width should gradually narrow as the clubshaft gets shorter, so that with the short irons the outside of each heel is about even with each armpit. Spacing your feet properly will allow your legs and hips the freedom of motion to work as they should, while also preventing you from swaying on the backswing.

After you've got your feet correctly positioned, you need to attain the proper amount of bend at the waist and knees. First, the knees: Stand straight, feet properly divided, then flex your knees slowly, looking down and watching until your kneecaps are directly above the instep of each foot. Next, bend at the waist while relaxing your arms and allowing them to hang slightly outward and away from your body. Let your buttocks slide backward slightly until your weight is resting comfortably on the balls of your feet, divided evenly between the left and right foot. Imagine you are standing on two large scales, one foot on each, with each registering half your weight.

Now waggle a little to get comfortable. You should feel that you are in a "ready" position, prepared to make a controlled yet powerful athletic motion. It's a similar position to that of a ten-

Your stance should be about as wide as your shoulders or slightly wider.

For good posture, bend at the waist and flex the knees slightly, allowing the relaxed arms to hang slightly outward and away from the body.

nis player waiting to receive a serve, a baseball infielder readying to see if a ball will be hit to him, or a hockey goalie anticipating a shot on goal.

Posture will vary slightly from player to player. Some prefer to flex more at the knees and hips and extend their arms further from the body, while others feel more comfortable standing straighter and holding the hands closer. Generally, the shorter the shaft, the closer your hands will be to your body. Monitor your hand position by making sure that your left hand is between one and two fist-widths away from your thigh.

Standing too upright or bending too much at either the knees or hips will cause problems. An upright stance will result in a high center of gravity, which can cause you to lose your balance toward the toes, causing shanked irons and heeled drives; or toward the heels, causing weak shots off the toe. An overly upright address can also result in an outside-in swing path and a vertical swing plane that employs too much arm action and not enough body turn.

Bending too much, on the other hand, can result in an inside-out swing path and a too-flat swing plane, neither of which is desirable.

Stand farther from the ball and position your hands farther from your body when playing longer shafted clubs, like the driver.

Short-shafted clubs, like the pitching wedge, require that you stand closer to the ball and position your hands closer to your body.

ALL ABOUT ALIGNMENT

Visualization can really help in the *alignment* of the swing. Golf is a target sport—you should have a target in mind whenever you set up to hit a shot, be it the fairway, the green, or the hole itself. Your ability to hit the ball to the chosen target depends on the correct alignment of both your body and the clubface. No matter how good your swing is, you won't hit the ball where you want it to go if your body and clubface aren't aligned correctly. There are a couple of reasons for this.

First, if either your body or clubface alignment is askew, you won't be aiming at the target, so the ball obviously won't go in that direction. You can't expect a bullet to hit a bullseye if the gun isn't aimed at it.

Second, if your body alignment and clubface alignment are out of sync with each other, the clubface will impart sidespin on the ball at impact, making the ball curve. Clockwise spin will make the shot curve from left to right. How much curve depends upon how much sidespin is put on the ball. A little clockwise spin results in a slight bend to the right, known as a *fade*. A lot of clockwise spin results in a left-to-right curve, called a *slice*. Conversely, counterclockwise spin will cause the shot to bend in the opposite direction—from right to left. A little counter-

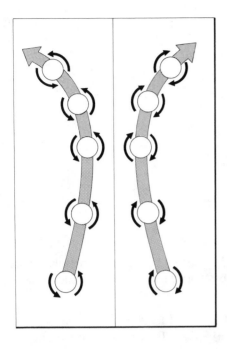

A ball spinning in a clockwise direction will curve from left to right, while a ball spinning counterclockwise will curve from right to left.

clockwise spin creates a slight bend, called a *draw*; a lot of spin results in a big curve, called a *hook*. (There will be more on how to curve the ball intentionally in either direction in chapter 8, Shotmaking.)

Obviously, neither a slice nor a hook is desirable (unless you need to curve the shot intentionally to get the ball around trouble and to the target), since the more a shot bends, the harder it is to control. In addition, a slice does not go nearly as far as a straighter shot, and a hook tends to run wildly after landing.

THE TARGET LINE

Your first step to achieving sound alignment is understanding what the *target line* is.

The target line is the imaginary line that runs straight from your ball to the target. The manner in which you set the lines of your body (feet, hips, shoulders) and the leading edge of the clubface should always relate to the target line.

Body Alignment

There are three ways to align your body to the target line: Square, open or closed. Square alignment means that your feet, hips and shoulders are parallel to the target line. To open the stance, shift

The target line is the imaginary line that runs straight from the ball to the target.

your body so the lines slant left of the target line. To close the stance, shift your body lines so they slant to the right of the target line. How open or closed your stance is depends on how far you shift your body away from being parallel to the target line. For example, shifting it slightly left means you're slightly open, while shifting it a great deal left means your stance is very open.

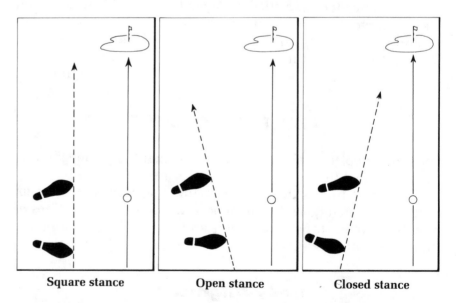

Square stance   **Open stance**   **Closed stance**

If the lines of your body—feet, hips and shoulders—are parallel to the target line, your stance is square *(left)*. If your body lines point left of the target line, your stance is open *(center)*. If your body lines point right of the target line, your stance is closed *(right)*.

Poor body alignment, one of the most common faults among amateur golfers, is extremely damaging. No matter how sound your swing mechanics may be, you'll never be an accurate player if your body alignment is poor because you aren't aiming at the target, although you think you might be.

What makes body alignment tricky is that it can be difficult to tell where your body lines are pointing when you are standing at address. You can check your alignment when practicing by first sighting a target, then laying a club down about a foot outside your toes so the shaft points directly at the target, paralleling the target line. Now you've got a concrete image in front of you to compare your body alignment with. Ignore the club on the ground, take a look at the target, and then try to assume a square stance. After you've settled into your address position, check your alignment against the clubshaft to see if you have unintentionally been setting up misaligned. If you have, adjust your stance to the desired position.

But what do you do when you're on the course and need help with your alignment? It's against the rules to lay a club down while playing a round. To give yourself an alignment aid, first stand behind the ball and visualize the target line running from the ball to the target. Next, find something specific that lies on the target line a few feet in front of the ball—it can be a leaf or a divot mark, anything that you can lock in on with your eyes to use as an intermediate target. As you step up to the ball, you should be able to see both the ball and the intermediate target you've just picked out in your field of vision. Imagine a line

For a concrete image to check your alignment against while practicing, lay a "pointer club" down on the ground parallel to your target line.

Pick out an intermediate target a few feet ahead of the ball as an aid to aiming correctly.

running between them, and line up in relation to it. Although you aren't able to lay a club down, you have, in essence, done the same thing by giving yourself a reference to line up with.

Body alignment is an element that must be monitored frequently. If you attend a professional tournament and stop by the practice range, odds are good that you'll see at least one player hitting shots while using a club on the ground parallel to the target line as a reference point. The pros know that good body alignment is essential, and that it's important to check it often to make sure it doesn't slip out of whack.

Clubface Alignment

How your clubface is aligned behind the ball is also crucial to accuracy. The clubface can be either square, open or closed. A *square* clubface means it is perpendicular to the target line, and thus aimed straight at the target. An *open* clubface points to the right of the target, while a *closed* clubface points left of the target. Though clubface alignment sounds simple, it's possible that yours may be off slightly without your realizing it, which will cost you accuracy. Remember, the difference between a few degrees of the angle of the clubface at impact can result in yards of difference between your intended target and where the ball actually finishes.

Again, make use of an intermediate target a few feet in front of the ball as a reference point to aim the clubface. Focus on pointing the leading edge of the face in the direction you desire, and take care not to disrupt the alignment while waggling the club.

If you're not sure whether your clubface is square or not, an

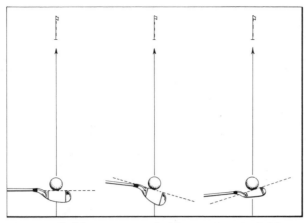

Square Clubface   Open Clubface   Closed Clubface

When the clubface is square, it is perpendicular to the target line and points directly at the target *(left)*; an open clubface points right of the target *(center)*; a closed clubface points left of the target *(right)*.

excellent way to check it is to lay a ruler flat on the ground behind the ball, perpendicular to the target line. That will give you a sharp visual guide to check your clubface alignment against and help you get used to resting the club squarely behind the ball.

The Perfect Alignment System

Here is a simple three-step system that will allow you to get your body and clubface perfectly aligned every time.

Step 1: Stand a few feet behind the ball and pick out an intermediate target approximately three to five feet in front of the ball.

Step 2: Position the clubhead behind the ball so the clubface points squarely at the intermediate target, perpendicular to the target line.

Step 3: Step into your address position using *both* the leading edge of the clubface and the imaginary line between the intermediate target and the ball (the target line) as reference points to assume either a square, open or closed stance, depending on the type of shot you plan to hit.

Note: Once you have aligned your clubface and body be careful that you don't accidentally slip out of alignment as you waggle into a ready position.

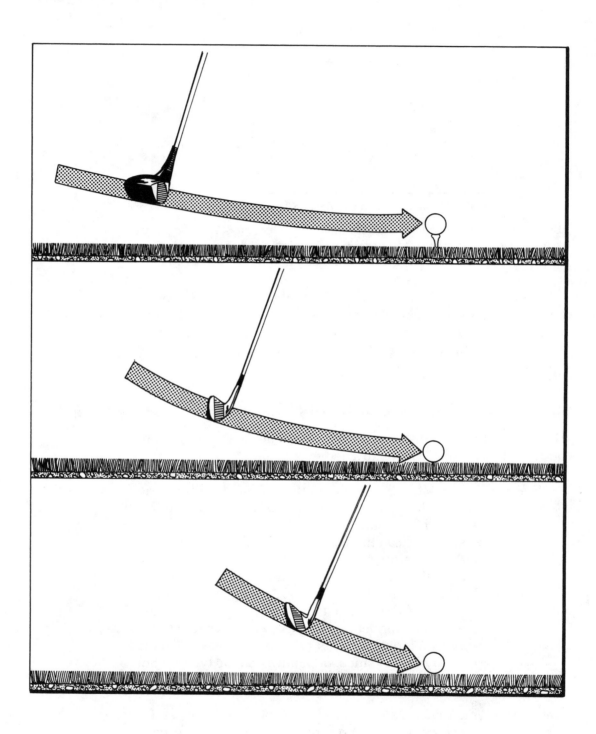

MAKING THE MOTION

There is no perfect golf swing. Every swing is different, even the good ones. Lee Trevino, Jack Nicklaus, Tom Watson, Curtis Strange and Arnold Palmer all can be identified by the way they swing at a golf ball because they all look a little different. But each one gets the job done. There are, however, certain common denominators found in every good swing that you should be aware of and work to incorporate into your own. If one or more of these elements is lacking, you won't strike the ball as well as you're capable.

THE START OF THE SWING: PROPER TAKEAWAY

The start of the swing is known as the *takeaway*, so called because the motion begins when you take the clubhead away from the ball. A good takeaway is smooth and unhurried, not a quick jerk of the club. It should be a unified, coordinated, "one-piece" action, with all parts of the body—arms, upper body, legs—working together, not separately. This is best achieved by putting the large muscles of the upper body to work: Keeping the left arm firm but not stiff, start the clubhead moving by turning your shoulders and shifting your weight gently to the inside of your right foot. Keep the clubhead low to the ground for the first few feet it travels away from the ball, by using your body to move it, not with a flip of the hands and wrists. Keep the arms and forearms relaxed but "quiet." An excellent way to achieve a one-piece takeaway while keeping the wrists and forearms from getting too active is to key on the triangle formed by your hands and two shoulders. Concentrate on keeping that triangle intact until the clubhead has traveled at least eighteen inches away from the ball; then let the right elbow bend inward and the wrists begin cocking.

A big advantage to using your whole body to make the takeaway is that it makes it easier to keep the motion slow and steady at the very start. A common fault in golf is a fast backswing; you can avoid this problem by striving to make a slow, smooth takeaway. Be especially conscious of doing this when there's pressure on, because nervousness will almost always cause a player to make a faster backswing. If you can keep the pace of the takeaway under control, you can usually keep the pace of the entire swing under control.

Before starting the takeaway it's very helpful to visualize the path you want the clubhead to take, then move it away from the

At address, imagine that your hands, left shoulder and right shoulder are three points of a triangle. Then shift the triangle to your right to execute a unified, one-piece takeaway.

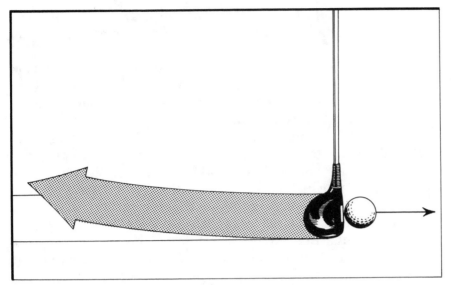

The clubhead should move back slightly to the inside on the takeaway to set up a good backswing path.

ball along that path, low to the ground. Picture a line that slants slightly to the inside, then make the clubhead follow it. You may find that you automatically make a one-piece takeaway simply by concentrating on moving the clubhead back low along the chosen line.

It's important that the clubhead moves only *slightly* inside, since the path it takes at the very start of the backswing helps determine the rest of the backswing path. If the takeaway path is too far inside, an inside-out swing path will result; taking the club away on a straight line, on the other hand, sets up an outside-in swing path. Neither is desirable.

THE FORWARD PRESS

The takeaway *must* be a slow, even motion. However, after you settle into a motionless address position, it can be difficult to get the club moving without starting with an abrupt jerk. If you have particular trouble with this, try making a *forward press*. A forward press is a slight, incidental motion that has no bearing on the swing, but is simply performed to start the gears of the takeaway turning. It will help you to release any pent-up physical tension beforehand so you can start the clubhead moving away from the ball in an even and unhurried fashion. Following are some examples of the forward press which you may want to try:

- Kick the right knee slightly inward (toward the left knee) before starting the clubhead back. Gary Player is known for this one.
- An extremely subtle forward press is to hold the club very lightly at address, and then when you're ready to start the swing, increase your grip pressure slightly before beginning the takeaway. Be sure not to squeeze the club tightly, however. You may want to perform this forward press with only one of the hands; Jack Nicklaus does it with his left.
- Move your hands forward slightly (toward the target). Be sure to move them only a fraction; otherwise you may upset your clubface alignment and/or create a bad angle with your right wrist.
- Twist your hips a fraction counterclockwise.
- Swivel your chin a small amount to the right. Another one of Nicklaus's.

You can invent your own forward press, but be very careful that it doesn't in any way upset your alignment or swing. Of course, you don't have to use a forward press at all; many good players don't. But if you feel uncomfortable when it comes to starting the swing, you may want to experiment with one.

CORRECT WEIGHT SHIFT

Shifting your weight properly on the backswing and downswing is essential to building maximum clubhead speed and maintaining balance throughout the swing.

As you swing back, your weight should follow the clubhead, gradually shifting to your right foot. The transfer begins immediately as you start the takeaway and ends when you've reached the top of the backswing, when approximately 90% of your weight is balanced firmly on the *inside* of the right foot. Don't let the weight move to the outside of the foot or your upper body will shift with it, causing a fault known as a "sway." You can guard against swaying not only by staying on the inside of the right foot at the top, but also by keeping your right knee flexed and firm, so it acts as a brace. You should feel slight pressure or strain in your right thigh as you reach the top, indicating that the right leg is doing its job as a brace.

Once you've reached the top of the backswing, the first downward move should be to shift the weight to the left foot, then follow by letting the upper body uncoil and the arms swing. It's the same kind of lower body–upper body sequence that oc-

Keep the right knee flexed and firm to act as a brace against "swaying" on the backswing.

curs naturally when throwing a ball: First you push off your back foot and step forward, then you sling your arm forward, not vice versa. However, many golfers, anxious to hit the ball hard, make the mistake of starting the downswing with the upper body, an error that results in poor downswing path and loss of power. This is often referred to as being "too quick."

HIP AND SHOULDER TURN

A scientific study of the golf swing performed by Centinela Hospital and Medical Center in Inglewood, California, the official hospital of the PGA and LPGA tours, determined that most of the power generated in the downswing comes from the large muscles in the chest and the back, the pectoralis major and the latissimus dorsi. They expend the most energy during what's termed the "acceleration phase," which starts about halfway through the downswing when the clubshaft reaches the point when it's approximately parallel to the ground.

In order to get into the proper position to let the "pecs" and "lats" do their jobs, it's crucial that you make a good body turn with your hips and shoulders on the backswing. After you've made a good turn, you'll be in the ready position to kick your weight toward the target and unwind your shoulders powerfully so the club is already moving downward fast and freely when it reaches the acceleration phase, where the pecs and lats can take charge and fire it through the hitting zone.

Making a good turn is easier if you concentrate on turning the hips and shoulders around a fixed point, such as your spine. Trying to keep your spine still while rotating your shoulders around it will not only result in a better upper body turn, but will also help eliminate swaying during the swing, increasing your chances of returning the clubface squarely to the ball.

Here are some possible keys to focus on to achieve a full backswing turn:

- Swivel your right hip back as far as you can.
- Move your left shoulder underneath your chin.
- Turn your back to the target.
- Turn so your belt buckle faces away from the target.
- Swing your hands into a position above your right shoulder at the top.

A word of caution here: When a player tries to extend his turn, it often leads to either a sway or a reverse weight shift. To prevent these errors, make sure to keep the right leg braced and the weight balanced securely on the inside of the right foot at the top of the backswing.

Also, keep the left arm firm. It doesn't have to be ramrod straight, but allowing it to collapse can cause the clubshaft to dip below parallel and the weight to fall back toward the left side at the top.

One way to achieve a full body turn is to concentrate on turning your back to the target.

THE DOWNSWING

The first move of the downswing must be the shifting of the weight from the right side to the left side, followed by the uncoiling of the shoulders. In other words, the hips should always move before the shoulders at the start of the downswing. As you swing the club downward, the inside of the upper part of your left arm should remain close to your left side, and your right elbow should return to your right side and "ride" close to your right hip. As long as these two things occur, you'll be able to use the power of your right side without fear of disrupting the downswing path.

Also on the downswing, make sure to keep the angle of your spine constant. Because it is the axis that the shoulders rotate around, raising or lowering the spine on the downswing will shift the downswing path of the clubhead. Either you'll hit the shot fat if you lower the spine or thin if you raise it.

THE HITTING ZONE

The *hitting zone* is the very bottom of the swing arc, about two feet before the club reaches the ball and two feet after impact.

This part of the swing is crucial, because if the clubhead is traveling on the proper path and releases through the hitting zone, the shot will be a good one. You can't do very much to manipulate the club through the hitting zone since it is moving so fast, but to keep it on the proper path you can key on keeping your head behind the ball through impact. Take care, though, not to let this inhibit the shifting of your weight to the left side.

THE FOLLOW-THROUGH

When you've reached the follow-through, the point after the clubhead has exited the hitting zone and the shaft is pointing at about three o'clock, the ball is gone. Thus the follow-through has no bearing on the shot itself. However, by making an effort to get into a good follow-through position, you will have had to have done the right things on the downswing and through the hitting zone. In the follow-through, you should strive for the following: Your right arm is extended straight toward the target; the inside of your upper left arm is still close to your left side; your head is still back behind where the ball had been resting; and about 80% of your weight is on your left foot.

Address: Relaxed and ready.

Takeaway: The swing starts with a one-piece takeaway, the clubhead staying low to the ground.

Halfway back: Weight is shifting smoothly to the right side, the right elbow folding close by the right hip.

At the top: Full hip and shoulder turn, weight braced on the inside of the right foot.

Halfway down: Legs driving toward the target with the right elbow riding close to the right hip.

Into the hitting zone: Head stays behind the ball; the left side remains firm while the right side exerts power.

Through impact: Head remains behind where the ball was; inside of upper left arm stays snug to the chest.

Follow-through: Right arm extended straight toward the target; momentum is starting to pull the left arm away from the chest and the head up.

Finish: Weight is balanced on the left side; head is up; back has released; hands are high over the left shoulder.

THE FINISH

Like the follow-through, the finish doesn't have any bearing on the shot itself. A good finish position, however, is an indicator that you have made a good downswing. Also, a poor finish can supply clues about the errors made that landed you there.

In a good finish, your momentum should carry you into a position where your weight is balanced firmly on your left side with the left leg straight. Your back should also be straight, your head up and your chest facing slightly left of the target.

Professional golfers and teachers have recently recognized the importance of releasing the back and allowing it to straighten as the body reaches the finish position, rather than holding the head back so the back bends into what's known as a "reverse C" position, which puts a great deal of strain on the back and can cause injury. If you have this habit, you can break it by consciously straightening your back after you reach the finish position. Keep reminding yourself to do it until the move blends into the end of your finish and you are releasing your back without having to think about it. At the finish your hands should be over your left shoulder.

TIMING

Timing is the synchronization of actions that take place as the swing progresses. Good timing is essential to maintaining a sound swing path and building maximum clubhead speed.

Remember that you swing the club with your body. From your feet to your fingers, each part plays some kind of role in bringing the club back and swinging it through in an efficient manner. Good timing involves knowing when to activate certain parts of the body.

The key thing to remember concerning timing is that you have to shift your weight to your left side with a strong motion of the hips before starting the downswing with the upper body. There should not, however, be a noticeable lag between these two actions—instead the upper body should immediately follow the lower body in "bang-bang" fashion. Imagine that one end of a long string is tied to your left knee and the other end to the butt end of the club. When you kick your weight off your right foot toward your left side, your left knee will slide toward your target, pulling the club/upper body behind it. That's the sensation you want to feel—that the upper body is slightly trailing the lower body. If the upper body gets ahead of the lower body, you'll swing the club down on an outside-in swing path, resulting in a pull to the left or a pull-slice. The error is known as "hitting from the top," and is a common fault among high-handicap golfers. It also springs up frequently when a player is trying to hit the ball a little harder than usual. If you face a situation in which you want to build more clubhead speed than usual, be sure to initiate the downswing with the lower body instead of getting too anxious and hitting from the top.

RHYTHM AND TEMPO

Contrary to what many golfers believe, rhythm and tempo are not the same thing. *Rhythm* has to do with the evenness of the motion. Imagine the rhythmic motion of a child on a swing—there is a gradual building of speed through the bottom of the arc before the child slowly comes to a peak and changes direction again.

Some players, such as Sam Snead and Ian Woosnam, exemplify just such a rhythmic motion when they swing. But a swing doesn't have to be particularly rhythmic to be effective: Ben Hogan, Arnold Palmer and Paul Azinger are all examples of slashing-type swingers.

Tempo is the elapsed time it takes from the instant the swing starts to the instant it is finished. For example, Tom Watson swings the club back and through in a crisp, businesslike fashion —his tempo is relatively quick. Payne Stewart, in contrast, has a slower backswing and builds clubhead speed more gradually on the downswing; therefore his tempo is slower than Watson's. This is not to say that players with slower tempo don't build as much clubhead speed as those with faster tempo; it's just that because they build it more gradually, the motion appears more effortless and somehow not as powerful. This is an illusion, as anyone who has ever seen either Snead, Stewart or Woosnam drive a golf ball, will attest.

Every golfer has a natural rhythm and tempo that he feels most comfortable with. The best way to find yours is to go to the practice range and hit at least a hundred wedge shots. Concern yourself only with the flow of the swing and making solid contact. Relax and rid your body of tension so you can feel your rhythm.

Return to this drill if you ever reach a point when you feel your rhythm is out of whack.

BALL POSITION

There are two schools of thought regarding where you play the ball in your stance. One prescribes that you play the ball in the same place—opposite the left heel—no matter what club you are hitting. The belief is that, for the sake of consistency, it is easier on the player if he doesn't have to worry about moving it around.

The second school of thought recommends varying where you play the ball in your stance depending on the club you use, so that woods and long irons are played off the left heel, short irons just ahead of center, and middle irons about midway between center and the left heel. This school believes that it's easier to make contact with the ball as the shaft gets shorter by playing it farther back in your stance, and with the shorter irons, that it's easier to hit the ball with a descending blow by playing it back instead of forward off the left heel.

Which school is correct? Both, since there are fine players who subscribe to either one. Keeping the ball in one constant position is simpler, whereas with the second you'll have to keep an eye out to monitor that you haven't accidentally allowed the ball to move too far forward or back in your stance, depending on the club. Many casual players prefer the second, however, because they feel that playing the ball farther back in their stance with shorter-shafted clubs makes it easier to make solid contact. You'll have to experiment to find which is right for you.

SAME SWING, DIFFERENT CLUB

One final, very important point to make to conclude the chapter on swinging is that, despite the fact that you use various different clubs to hit shots of different distances throughout the course of a given round, the motion that you make should be essentially the same. Of course, the lengths of the shafts will force you to stand at different distances from the ball, and the shorter the shaft, the steeper the downswing angle will be. But that will take care of itself. If you have developed good swing mechanics, you should simply concern yourself with setting up properly in relation to the ball and pulling the trigger, repeating the same swing no matter what club you have in your hands.

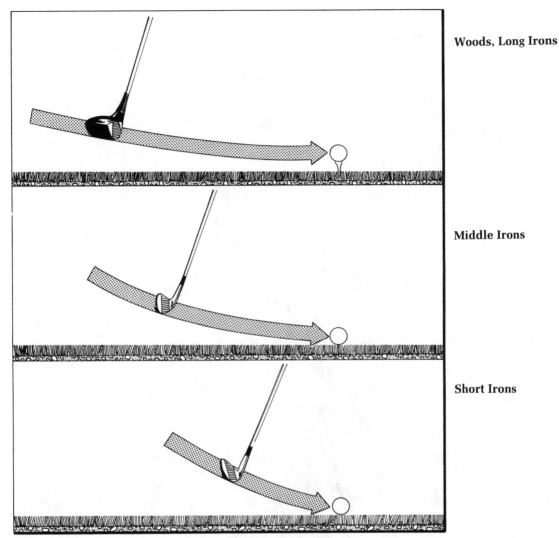

Woods, Long Irons

Middle Irons

Short Irons

Downswing angles will naturally vary depending on the length of the club-shaft. Woods and long irons will approach the ball on a shallow angle *(top)*; middle irons on a medium angle *(center)*; and short irons on a sharp, descending angle *(bottom)*.

TROUBLESHOOTING YOUR SWING

The golf swing is a complex action. To produce a decent shot, the clubhead must be swung on a precise path at a relatively high speed. Although it may seem very difficult to swing well, it's certainly not impossible as long as you understand what you're doing, why you're doing it, and have learned to execute it correctly.

To hit the ball well, you need to swing the club on the proper swing path in order to return the clubface squarely to the ball at impact. The role of the backswing is to set the club and your body in the best possible position to make a good downswing. The position you reach at the top of the backswing is extremely important and deserves your strict attention.

AT THE TOP

There are three mechanical points that occur at the top of the backswing that directly affect the downswing, and therefore the way you make contact with the ball. They are:
1. Clubface position—square, open or closed.
2. Clubshaft alignment in relation to the ground—parallel, short of parallel or past parallel.
3. Clubshaft alignment in relation to your body lines—"down the line," "laid off" or "crossing the line."

CLUBFACE POSITION

At the top of the backswing, the clubface can be either square, open or closed, depending on the position of your left hand and wrist.

If the clubface is square at the top, then the back of your left hand will be approximately square with the back of your left wrist, and from there, an active release of the hands on the downswing will result in squaring the clubface correctly through impact, producing a straight shot.

An open clubface at the top is caused when the left hand is bent so the back of the hand and the wrist form a concave angle. Golfers with a lot of physical strength sometimes prefer to have an open clubface at the top, because from there they can release the hands as aggressively as they want without having to worry about closing the face before impact and causing a hook. However, the average player will have trouble getting the clubface back to a square position if it is open at the top. Thus, the face will be open at impact, causing the shot to go to the right.

The opposite happens when the clubface is closed at the top —the left hand is bent downward so it forms a convex angle with the wrist. Releasing the hands from this position closes the face even more before impact, resulting in a shot that goes well to the left.

A square clubface position at the top is achieved when the back of the left hand and the left wrist are square with each other.

If the back of the left hand and wrist form a concave angle at the top, the clubface is in an open position.

The clubface is closed at the top if the back of the left hand and wrist form a convex angle.

If you are having trouble with the direction of your shots, it may be a problem with clubface position at the top. The best way to determine this is to get someone to stand behind you as you're hitting shots and observe the position of your left hand and wrist when you reach the top of the backswing. Another option is to use a video camera to record your swing so that you can analyze your position for yourself .

If you detect a problem with clubface position, you must marry the adjustment you make in your hand position with the proper visual image of what is happening at the top. The more closely you can associate a picture of proper clubface position with the *feeling* of proper position, the quicker and more efficiently you'll be able to incorporate it into your muscle memory.

Bear in mind that if a change is needed it may not be easy to make. As with any swing flaw, you are substituting a bad habit with a good one, and bad habits are sometimes hard to break. To put it another way, when you make a swing change, you are substituting a new feeling for an old, comfortable feeling, and that's never easy, even though the old, comfortable feeling is incorrect.

Whenever you make a mechanical adjustment or change in your swing, you must think of the new feeling as a physical *cue* that you are performing the change. Here's an example: A high handicapper is striking the ball inconsistently because he sways well to the right on the backswing, so his weight is on the outside of his right foot at the top. To eliminate the sway, the physical cue he chooses is a feeling of firmness in the right knee coupled with the feeling that his weight is braced against the inside of his right foot at the top.

If you can visualize a picture of the change you are making and associate it with the cue, then you can help institute the change even when you aren't practicing. When you find yourself with a moment to daydream, visualize what you look like at the top of the swing, with your clubface in the new corrected position, while at the same time remembering what it feels like to achieve this position. Even though you aren't swinging a club, by doing this you are still helping to familiarize yourself with the swing change.

Overswinging

Another very common fault among handicap golfers is allowing the clubshaft to dip below the point where it is parallel to the line of the ground, known as *overswinging*. (Note: Overswinging isn't usually a problem among senior and heavyset players, who generally lack the flexibility needed to swing the club past parallel.)

A player may make a very long backswing because he believes that the farther back he can wind the club, the faster he'll be able to swing it through on the downswing. Unfortunately, once the backswing gets to be a certain length, you reach a point of diminishing returns. Overswinging can lead to other swing

Overswinging—when the club-shaft passes the point of being parallel to the ground—can lead to several faults, including reverse weight shift and loss of club control.

flaws, such as loss of clubhead control, reverse weight shift to the left foot, excessive upper-body movement, and a breakdown in good hand and wrist position.

Often a player doesn't realize he is swinging past parallel. Instead, he wrongly equates the feeling he has at the peak of the backswing with the vision of the clubshaft parallel to the ground. What he feels is not what's actually happening. (Remember: "What you feel is not always what's real.") To the player who overswings without realizing it, stopping the shaft at parallel will feel like a three-quarter swing. To cure the problem, he needs to get what he feels in sync with what is actually happening.

To determine if you're overswinging, have a friend face you and observe your swing to determine where your clubshaft is at the top. Also have him check for any of the above-mentioned swing flaws that often happen with overswinging.

If you find that you have a problem with overswinging, you must learn to associate the proper image of what is happening with what you *feel*. The best way, once again, is to associate a physical signal with the visual image of a parallel position at the top.

First, you have to stop the backswing at parallel and determine what that feels like. No doubt you will feel as if you are making a short, incomplete backswing. Find a physical *cue*, or signal, that tells you when you've reached that point. Some examples of such cues might be:

- The left shoulder has swiveled underneath the chin.
- The weight is fully "loaded" on the inside of the right foot.
- The right hip has turned as far back as possible while keeping the weight balanced on the right foot.
- The weight of the clubshaft is supported by the left thumb.
- Your back is facing the target.

When you've found a cue that you're comfortable with, concentrate on associating it with the visual image of yourself swinging a driver to a parallel position at the top of your backswing. Once you've discovered one that you're comfortable with, you can practice associating the cue with the picture at any time —even when you aren't on the course or practicing. In fact, the more you do it, the sooner you'll be able to break the old habit of overswinging.

Again, bear in mind that old habits such as overswinging won't be easy to break, because ingrained, comfortable physical feelings are difficult to abandon. But if you truly want to improve,it will be worth the effort.

Clubshaft Alignment

At the top of the backswing, the direction that the clubshaft points plays a major role in determining what kind of downswing path the clubhead will take.

Assuming that you've set up in a square position, if the clubshaft is parallel to the target line at the top of the backswing, then you are in the best possible position. Ideally the clubhead will approach the ball on a slightly inside path, the clubface will strike the ball squarely, and then the clubhead will swing through on a slightly inside path as it proceeds forward into the follow-through. This is known as an inside-square-inside downswing path, which every player should strive for.

If the shaft points *down the line* at the top of your backswing so it is parallel to the lines of your feet, hips and shoulders at address, you are putting it in the best possible position to set up an inside-square-inside path.

If, however, the clubshaft at the top points to the right of your body lines, you are making an error known as *crossing the line*. If you swing the shaft across the line at the top, you are setting up an inside-out downswing path, which can produce anything from hooked to pushed shots, depending on the angle of the clubface at impact. The opposite of crossing the line is called *laying off,* when the shaft points left of your body lines,

Ideally, the path the club-head travels during the downswing should be from slightly inside, then square to the target line at impact, then back to the inside after impact.

If the clubshaft points *down the line* at the top, it is in the best possible position to set up a proper inside-square-inside downswing path.

setting up an outside-in downswing path that leads to pulls and pull-slices. If you have a problem with these types of shots, have a friend check your clubshaft alignment at the top.

Crossing the Line

If you determine that you are crossing the line, the first thing you should check is to see if you are taking the clubhead away too abruptly to the inside. If you are, adjust your takeaway path so the clubhead moves only slightly to the inside.

Be aware that it is possible to have a good takeaway path yet still cross the line at the top. The cause is sloppy wrist action at the top, and the cure is to firm up your grip pressure to cut down on excess motion and keep the club on line.

The best cue to concentrate on to change clubshaft alignment at the top is your left thumb. If your grip is sound, the left thumb should be underneath the shaft at the top of the backswing, supporting the weight of the club. The direction your thumb points is also the direction the shaft points. So by pointing your left thumb slightly to the left at the top (again, have someone help you determine when the shaft is pointing down the line) you'll be able to adjust your shaft alignment to a more suitable position. To change the direction your thumb points, you'll need to change the position of your left wrist. That feeling is your cue

Crossing the line occurs when the clubshaft points to the right of your body lines at the top, setting up an inside-out downswing path.

that your clubshaft alignment is down the line at the top, so practice associating that feeling with the image of swinging the clubshaft into a down-the-line position at the top.

Laying Off

If, on the other hand, the clubshaft points left of the target line at the top, you are making an error known as *laying off*. Again, laying off sets up a poor downswing path, this time from outside-in, causing either a pull or a pull-slice, depending on what the clubface angle is at impact. If either of these shots appears often in your game, check to see if you're laying the club off at the top. If so, first check to see if you are taking the clubhead away from the ball on too straight of a line. Remember, the clubhead must move slightly to the inside as you start back; otherwise you'll encourage an upright swing plane and a laid-off position at the top. If this is your problem, start the clubhead moving on an inside path at the takeaway while concentrating on keeping your right elbow close to your right hip until the clubshaft is past the nine-o'clock position.

If your takeaway is good but you're still laying off at the top, use your left thumb as a cue to change the shaft alignment, this time pointing the thumb more toward the target (to the right).

Laying off occurs when the clubshaft points left of your body lines at the top, setting up an outside-in downswing path.

SOLVING OTHER SWING PROBLEMS

Since there are a lot of things going on between the start of the takeaway and the top of the finish, there's no doubt that a lot can go wrong with a golf swing. Although it's not likely that major flaws will suddenly occur in your swing, small faults can crop up from day to day, and if they go unchecked can escalate into big trouble.

It's fairly easy to tell if something's gone wrong in your swing because your shots will reflect it. Everyone will hit a bad shot now and then, but if you start detecting a pattern—repeatedly hitting a certain type of shot—you'd better try to find out where the glitch is. Here are some errors to check for, depending on the type of shot you're hitting. Remember, though, that it's not always easy to ferret out the exactly problem yourself. If that's the case, your next step should be to seek out a competent teaching pro to help you remedy the situation.

PULL

A *pull* is when the ball flies to the left of your intended target. There can be a number of causes.

First, make sure you aren't unintentionally aiming left of target. If so, you aren't really pulling the ball; you simply aren't aiming correctly.

If that's not the problem, look to see if you're playing the ball too far forward in your stance. In a perfect downswing path, the clubhead approaches the ball from slightly inside, then moves squarely down the target line for a brief instant when contact is made, then moves back to the inside.

A pull occurs when the club is moving inside the target line when contact is made, so the shot is "pulled" left of the target. If the ball is too far forward in the stance, the clubhead will make contact after it has squared itself to the target line, when it is moving back to the inside, causing the shot to go left.

If ball position isn't the problem, then you are swinging the club down on an outside-in path. This could be caused by an outside-in backswing, so check that you aren't taking the club away too far to the outside. Check also that your right elbow is gently folding and riding close to your right hip as you swing the club back. You may also be standing too close to the ball, forcing an upright, outside-in swing.

It is possible to have a good backswing, yet to swing down on an outside-in path. This can be caused by laying the clubshaft off the line at the top, which puts it in a position for an out-to-in downswing. It can also be caused by starting down with the upper body instead of the lower, in other words "hitting from the top." Another cause is failing to keep the right elbow close to the right hip on the downswing.

PUSH

A push occurs when the club is moving on an inside-out path in relation to the ball instead of inside-square-inside, so the shot flies straight right of the target. If you're hitting this type of shot, first check to see that you aren't actually misaligned and unintentionally aimed to the right of the target.

If alignment isn't the problem, next check that the ball isn't too far back in your stance. If it is, contact will be made while the clubhead is swinging from inside-out before it has had a chance to get square to the target line.

If the ball position is okay, then your problem is an inside-out downswing. First, check that you aren't swinging back too far inside on the takeaway. Stop your backswing when the shaft is at the nine-o'clock position to see if it is parallel to the target line, as it should be. If it is pointing right of the target line, you're swinging back too much on the inside.

It is possible to have a good backswing path and still make an inside-out downswing. One way is by allowing the shaft to cross the line at the top, which sets it into position for an in-to-out downswing path. Another way is to allow the inside of the upper left arm to move away from the left side on the downswing and through impact.

SLICE

A slice, a shot that bends severely from left to right, is the most common shot among amateur golfers. It occurs when the clubface is open in relation to the line the clubhead is moving on, so a great deal of clockwise spin is imparted on the ball, making it curve so much. For some reason, the golfer is not squaring the clubface to the ball at impact.

One reason for this could be that the grip position is too weak and needs to be strengthened. Another reason could be that the player is "blocking" the release of the hands and not allowing the right forearm to rotate over the left through impact, squaring the face to the ball. Too much tension in the left arm and wrist can cause this to happen.

Note that a slice can occur in conjunction with a pull or push, resulting in a pull-slice, which starts left of the target then bends back toward it, or a push-slice, which starts right of target and bends even farther right. If this is the case, you've got to solve the problems of both poor swing path and clubface position at impact.

HOOK

A hook is the opposite of a slice. Caused by a closed face at impact, it bends severely from right to left. In its worst form a hook can be very sharp, known as a "snap" hook or a "duck" hook, and can be more damaging than a slice because the ball dives hard left and nearly directly into the ground, stunting distance tremendously and possibly finding big trouble.

Closing the clubface too much before impact is often caused by having the hands in a position that's too strong on the grip, so your first attempt to correct the problem should be to check that your hands aren't turned too far to the right.

If your grip doesn't seem to be the problem, it could be that your right side is overpowering your left, so the left wrist and forearm "collapse" and the right hand rolls too quickly over the left instead of gradually. If this is your problem, check to see that you aren't standing too far from the ball, forcing you to reach too much and swing on a very flat plane, promoting a fast rolling action on the forearms on the downswing.

If, however, the problem isn't ball position, then you probably need to take a firmer grip with your left hand and pull the club down with the left arm, exerting a little less force on the downswing with the right side.

SKIED/FAT SHOTS

If you're popping your drives straight up or hitting the turf behind the ball, you're doing something that's shifting your swing arc downward on the downswing. Two common causes are bending at the waist or adding flex at the knees during the downswing, both of which can occur when you try to hit the ball too hard.

Another possible cause is a reverse weight shift—when the weight is shifted to the left on the backswing, then to the right on the downswing; or, when the weight is shifted to the right on the backswing, but not properly shifted to the left on the downswing.

Note that if you're skying only your drives, it could be that you're teeing the ball too high. It should be just high enough so that only about half the ball is above the top edge of the driver's face.

THIN/TOP

The opposite of a skied or fat shot is a thinned or topped shot. The swing arc is too high, so instead of hitting the ball flush with the clubface, you make contact with the ball with the bottom part of the clubface, producing a low, weak shot or a grounder that never gets airborne.

This is a common problem among beginners, usually caused by "lifting your head," or raising the spine angle while swinging the club down. Another cause is losing knee flex on the downswing, so the upper body lifts up and the swing arc is raised. Cure this by visualizing the spine as the axis the shoulders turn on, concentrating on keeping the axis still as the shoulders revolve back and through, swinging the club as they go.

Also note that if your chief problem with thin or topped shots is with your driver, it may be that you're teeing the ball too low.

Teeing the ball too high or low will result in poor drives. For best results, the ball's equator should be even with the top edge of the clubface when using a driver.

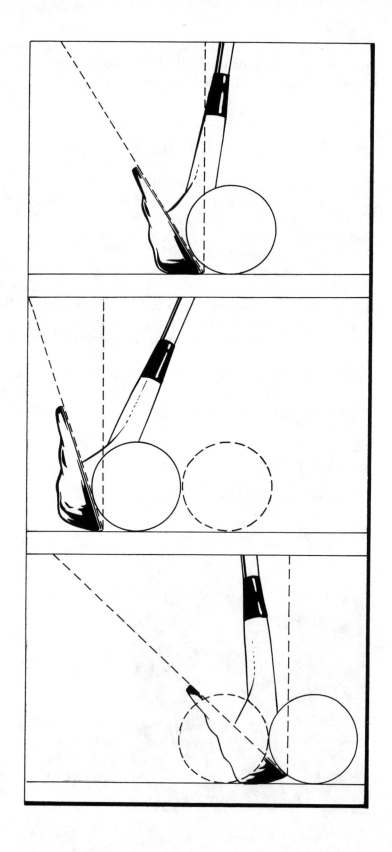

SHOTMAKING

Every golfer has what's known as a "natural shot," which is produced when a normal full swing is made without trying to make the ball do anything in particular. For example, if you take a 5-iron, set up square and simply try to make solid contact, the shot you hit will be your natural shot. In most cases it will be either a *draw*, which curves slightly from right to left, or a *fade*, which curves slightly from left to right. Very rarely will a player consistently hit the ball perfectly straight, with no hint of curve. The height the ball flies is also part of the natural shot. Some players, such as Greg Norman, hit the ball on a high, soft-landing trajectory, while others, like Paul Azinger, hit lower, harder shots.

Anytime a player tries to make the ball behave differently than it would from their natural shot, they are "shotmaking"— manufacturing a shot. Shotmaking is typically performed when the situation demands a shot different from the player's natural shot. For example, if your natural shot flies on a high trajectory, and you are driving into the teeth of a high headwind, it would be better to manufacture a lower shot that wouldn't be knocked down as much by the breeze. It's a fact that professional players are not only better ball-strikers than amateurs, but are also notably better at shotmaking. Though many weekend players understand the mechanics of hitting the ball higher or lower and bending it left or right, few have any real success at trying to play anything other than their natural shot. However, proper visualization will increase your ability to make the ball behave the way you want it to.

THE STRATEGY BEHIND FADES AND DRAWS

Why bend the ball? Why not try to hit it straight at the target every time? The answer is that it's too hard to hit the ball exactly straight every shot. Too many things have to be precise: Swing path has to be perfect, and the clubface must be aligned exactly at the target at the split-second of impact so that no sidespin is put on the ball and the shot flies perfectly straight. If, by accident, the clubface is open or closed by only a few degrees at impact, the shot could miss the target by five to fifteen yards, depending on what club was hit.

That's why it's logical to put some sidespin on the ball intentionally to make it curve in a specific direction. Though you won't always put exactly the same amount of spin on the ball every time, at least you'll know which direction the ball is going to move.

Planning for the ball to curve slightly in one direction or the other will increase your chances of putting the ball close to your target while decreasing your chances of finding trouble.

Here's an example. Imagine that you're standing on the tee of a tight, tree-lined fairway. Your plan is to aim down the right center of the fairway and play a draw. That way, if the ball curves to the left as planned, you'll end up safely in the center. If you accidentally put less sidespin on the shot than anticipated, the ball will fly relatively straight and still find the right-center of the fairway. If you accidentally put more drawspin on the shot than planned, it will curve a little more than expected, but still will land on the left side of the fairway. In all three cases, the ball will be on the short grass. The same principle applies to approach shots: When the ball bends a little more or less than expected, you'll still end up putting.

Here's another example, this one illustrating how working the ball helps take trouble out of play. Imagine that your ball lies in the middle of the fairway, 150 yards from the green. The pin is cut close to the right edge of the putting surface, and a large pond closely guards the right side of the green. You're down in your match and need to make a birdie, but if you try to hit a straight shot at the pin and lose the ball right, you could find the water. If your natural shot is a draw, attempting to shoot for the pin means aiming at the water and trying to work the ball back to the flag—a risky prospect. The better play is to aim left of the flag and manufacture a fade. That way, even if the ball curves a little more or less than you expect, you'll still end up on the green with an opportunity for birdie and at least an excellent chance for par, instead of in the hazard.

Another, more obvious value of shotmaking is being able to get the ball out of and around trouble. No golfer, no matter how accurate, can avoid trouble all the time. Having the ability to get the ball to the target by bending shots sharply around trees or punching it low under branches will save you a great number of strokes.

CLUBFACE ALIGNMENT, SPIN AND SHOT SHAPE

Before going into greater depth on shotmaking, it's important that you understand and are able to visualize exactly what happens when the clubface makes contact with the ball at impact— how the angle of the clubface can make the ball fly higher or lower than usual, or impart sidespin that makes the shot curve left or right.

As you swing the club downward, the clubhead rotates in a counterclockwise direction, so the toe rotates past the heel. If you set up squarely and make a theoretically perfect swing, the clubface would be precisely square to the target line at impact, the toe passing the heel so a slight amount of drawspin is put on the ball. To put additional drawspin on the ball to make it hook, or make it spin the opposite way to fade or slice, you need to adjust your body alignment and/or make other technical swing changes, adjusting the clubface angle and swing path to put the type of spin on the ball to produce the shot you need.

LEFT-TO-RIGHT SHOTS

The simplest way to hit a fade is to open your stance slightly in relation to the target line, keeping the clubface aimed squarely at the target; then swing normally. Turning your body into an open position shifts your swing path so that the clubhead moves on a slightly outside-in downswing path, imparting a slight amount of clockwise spin that results in a fade. The farther open you stand, the more the ball should bend from left to right.

If that adjustment alone isn't working for you, try keeping your left wrist firm and preventing your right hand from passing your left through impact, while visualizing the heel of the club leading the toe through the hitting zone.

You might also try standing about half an inch closer to the ball, which will force a more upright swing plane and promote an outside-in swing path.

By experimenting with one, two or all three of these adjustments, you should find success bending shots from right to left in varying degrees, from a little curve to a lot, even if you never have before.

RIGHT-TO-LEFT SHOTS

Just as you'll run into situations when a fade is the percentage shot, you'll also encounter times when a draw is needed. To manufacture a draw, keep the clubface aimed squarely at the target, but close your stance slightly; then swing normally. Closing the stance shifts the swing path so it is slightly inside-out, imparting counterclockwise spin on the ball to create a draw. The more closed your stance, the more the ball should curve.

If changing your stance alone isn't producing a draw, make a conscious effort to roll your right hand over your left through impact while visualizing the toe of the club quickly passing the heel as it sweeps through the bottom of the swing arc.

One other adjustment that promotes drawspin is setting up about half an inch farther away from the ball than usual. This results in a slightly flatter swing plane; the flatter the plane, the more inside-out the swing path will be, producing right-to-left spin.

VISUALIZATION AND
MAKING THE BALL BEND

When planning to curve the ball in a specific direction, the most important part of the shot to concentrate on is the middle, when it is curving most. If you want to hit a fade, get a clear picture of the ball peaking in its flight, then turning gently to the right and dropping downward. If a hook is what you need, focus sharply on the ball hanging in the air, then veering sharply left. The key is to concentrate on the part of the shot where the ball is bending in the direction you want it to.

HIGH AND LOW SHOTS

Sometimes you'll need to hit the ball on a higher or lower trajectory than normal to avoid obstacles, usually trees or tree limbs. The easiest way to alter the trajectory of a shot is to go either up or down a club, but occasionally you'll have to keep the ball extremely low or make it rise extremely quickly. Here's how to do both.

STAYING LOW

Imagine the following situation: You've driven the ball into trees on a short par four. Your lie is good and there is no trouble between the ball and the green, except the low hanging branches of a tree in front of you. The tree is too close to go over or around; however, if you can hit the ball very low and hard, you should be able to fire it under the limbs, landing it short of the green so it runs onto the surface.

Another case where a low shot is useful was mentioned above—when a strong headwind or crosswind blows. Typically, the wind blows even harder higher off the ground, so a high shot is even more susceptible to being shortened or blown left or right by a strong wind. The lower you can keep the shot, the less it will be affected by the wind.

Mechanics: Low Ball

To hit the ball on a lower trajectory than normal, you must make certain adjustments at address that will decrease the loft of the club. Do this by playing the ball one ball-width farther back in your stance, keeping the position of your hands normal so that now they are ahead of the ball. Keep the clubhead low on the backswing and make a shallow, sweeping swing—an abrupt backswing and downswing will cause the ball to rise more quickly. Make sure the hands stay ahead of the clubhead as you swing the club through the hitting zone. To hit a low draw, release your hands through impact. To make the ball fade, keep your left hand firm and don't allow your right hand to roll over your left until after you've struck the ball. Beware, though, that a fade is more difficult to hit low because fades naturally rise higher.

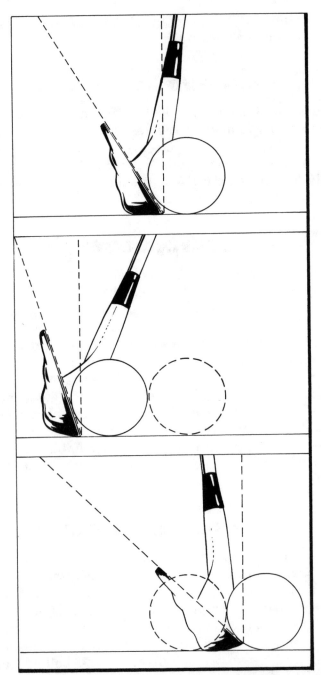

Positioning the ball normally in your stance so the sole of the club is flat on the ground will allow you to use the club's true loft *(top)*. To decrease the effective loft and hit the ball lower, move the ball back in your stance one ball-width while keeping your hands in the same position *(center)*. Likewise, moving the ball forward one ball-width increases the effective loft so the shot flies higher.

HITTING HIGH BALLS

There will be times when you wish to hit the ball on a higher trajectory than usual. The simplest way is to take a more lofted club. But suppose you're close to a tree and need to hit an even higher sand wedge than usual, or need the ball to rise very quickly. There are adjustments you can make to hit an even higher wedge than normal. Another instance when you might want to hit a higher shot is when there's a strong wind behind you on the tee.

Mechanics: High Wedge

Set up in an open stance, playing the ball about one ball-width farther forward than usual, your left hand even with the club-head, angling the face back and adding loft. Pick up the club abruptly on the backswing and keep your right hand from passing your left through impact to keep the clubface from closing, giving you maximum use of the loft. Strive to make your follow-through with your hands high.

Mechanics: High Drive

To hit a high drive tee, the ball slightly higher than usual, playing it about one-half of a ball-width farther forward and widening your stance by about an inch. Keep the clubhead very low on the takeaway and stay behind the ball through impact. These adjustments will produce a high tee shot that will ride a tailwind to give you additional yardage.

PART III

AROUND THE GREEN

PITCHING

The area ranging from about 70 yards to the pin is commonly called "the scoring zone," because it is there that a majority of shots can be saved—or lost. The more accurate you are with the short shots played in the scoring zone, the lower you'll score.

Visualization is crucial when playing short shots because pinpoint accuracy will pay big dividends by saving a lot of strokes. Of course, you should try to be accurate with all shots: When hitting a driver, your goal is to hit the fairway; when hitting a long approach, your goal is to hit the green. But when playing shorter shots—pitches and chips—your goal isn't just to get the ball on the green, but to stop it in the area close to the hole. To be successful at hitting such a small target you've got to control both the distance and direction of the shot precisely.

Not many golfers have the strength to boom a drive 300 yards or hit a 1-iron well, but anyone can have a good short game: It doesn't take that kind of natural ability to be good at pitching, chipping and putting. There are many good players who make up for a lack of length by developing a sharp short game. Visualization is crucial to planning and executing shots in the scoring zone, from pitches to chips to putts.

PITCHING: CONTROL IS THE KEY

A pitch is a shot ranging from about seventy to twenty yards—less than a full wedge, but more than a chip. The pitch is a difficult play because it demands that you control how far the ball goes by regulating the force of your swing. You don't have to worry about manipulating the distance for a full shot, in which you choose the proper club, swing back fully and pull the trigger, swinging down with about the same force every time. How far the shot goes depends on which club you used.

But when the ball lies inside the distance that you can hit a full wedge (usually about 90 yards or less for the average player), you must determine the force of the swing in order to hit the ball the desired distance. Being "distance accurate" while making less than a full swing is a skill that frustrates many amateur golfers. A recent study by Dave Pelz, an expert in the field of golf research, indicated that most amateurs hit their pitch shots with good direction, but have trouble hitting it the right distance. In other words, they're hitting the ball toward the pin most of the time, but usually end up too long or too short. By finding a way to be more precise with distance control, you could start sticking the ball closer to the hole with your pitches and getting down in two instead of three.

MECHANICS: BASIC PITCH

Brute force isn't essential to hitting a good pitch; solid contact is. Therefore, you should stress balance, rhythm and a steady upper body when hitting this shot. With a wedge, set up in a narrow, open stance (heels about one foot apart). Establish a low center of gravity for good balance by flexing your knees a little and distributing your weight evenly between the balls and heels of your feet, shading it toward the inside of your left foot. Ball position should be just ahead of center. Swing back by turning your shoulders around your stationary spine, allowing the wrists to cock naturally into a compact position, avoiding any excess, sloppy wrist action. Let the clubhead come to a controlled stop before swinging down with a smooth, rhythmic action, and finish with your weight on your left foot.

GAUGING DISTANCE

There's more than one way to gauge how far you hit a pitch shot. Here are some you can experiment with.

To hit a basic pitch, set up slightly open with the ball just forward of center and your weight shaded toward your left side.

Bring the club back by turning your shoulders; allow the wrists to cock quickly, keeping your spine stationary and your lower-body movement to a minimum.

For crisp contact, point your knees toward the target and keep your head down through impact.

Watch the Clock

One of the oldest, most effective visual aids for gauging pitching distance is to imagine that your left arm is a hand on a large clockface. The number your arm points to depends upon how far back you swing the club; the length of your backswing determines how much force you swing down with and in turn, how far the ball goes.

Let's get more specific about the image of the clock. To hit a full wedge, you most likely swing your left arm back so it points to about eleven o'clock, depending upon how flexible you are. With the clockface in mind, you can shorten your swing by specific increments by pointing your left arm to different positions between eight-thirty and eleven o'clock. That will give you six different lengths of backswing (eight-thirty, nine, nine-thirty, ten, ten-thirty, and eleven). By varying the length of your backswing by specific increments, you will also vary the length of your shots by specific increments.

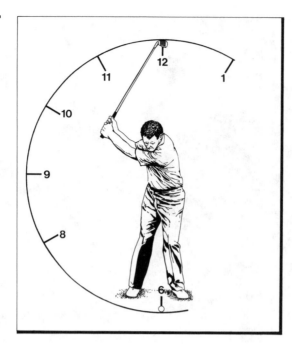

To help gauge the length of your backswing, and thus the distance the pitch goes, pretend that your left arm is a hand on a clockface, concentrating on pointing it to a specific number at the top of the backswing.

When hitting each shot, work on getting a clear vision of the clock and key on stopping your left arm so it points to the exact position on the face you desire. From there accelerate crisply through the ball.

Get Hip

Another way to gauge the length of your backswing on less-than-full wedge shots is to use your right hip as a reference point in determining how far back you swing your hands. For example, you can key on stopping your hands just below the level of your hip, even with the hip, just above it, or a little farther above it still.

It may prove more difficult to be as exacting with this method as it is with the idea of the clockface, but some players prefer it because it gives them a concrete reference point to work with. And since the hip is actually part of the body, you can "feel" the relationship between it and the hands in a more profound way.

Peak Performance

There is another way to determine how far you hit a pitch shot that is much less mechanical than the previous two methods while depending more on your ability to visualize.

With this method, you determine how far the ball will go by imagining how high you want the ball to peak in the air, then using "feel" to hit it hard enough so it peaks where you intend it to. The higher the ball peaks, the farther it carries and thus the longer it goes; by making the ball peak lower, you hit a shorter pitch. (Note that this method works only if you keep the angle of the clubface consistent on every swing—opening the face and adding loft to the club will obviously cause the ball to peak higher and fly shorter than normal.) The best reference point to use when determining how high the ball peaks is the top of the flagstick.

The same principle works for shooting a basketball: You sight the hoop, get a feel for how far away you are, visualize how high the ball should peak in order to reach the hoop, and then release the ball with enough force so it peaks where you had pictured it.

"Feel" the Distance

You may choose to determine the length of the shot not by measuring the length of backswing or predicting the peak of the trajectory, but by going by "feel" alone, which, if you practice enough, can be reliable.

You can compare it to putting. Most players don't think about how far back they are swinging the putterhead when they hit a putt; they simply allow their sense of feel to take over to determine the length and force of the stroke. The problem is that most casual players aren't familiar enough with their pitching swings in order to have the fine sense of feel needed to be consistently distance accurate using this method. (You probably make between 28 to 36 putts for every 18 holes you play, while hitting only four to 12 pitch shots. That alone tells you why your feel for distance is sharper with a putter than it is with a wedge.) That's why most handicap players will have better results employing a mechanically oriented method.

ALWAYS CALL YOUR PITCH

No matter how you decide to regulate the distance of your pitch shots, *always* be sure to visualize exactly how you want the shot to turn out. Imagine the click of the clubface on the ball, the shot rising in line with the pin, then landing close by. Did it bounce? Did it land beyond the pin, check up and spin back? Did the wind affect the trajectory? That's up to you and how you dreamed the shot to happen.

AIM HIGH, NOT LOW

A major fault of casual players is that they nearly always leave the ball short of the hole on every shot from approaches to putts. This is often chronically true with pitch shots. If you find that you're continually leaving the ball fifteen to twenty feet short, try visualizing the ball landing on top of the flagstick instead of hitting short of the pin and rolling up to the cup. The difference will be dramatic.

GETTING IT STRAIGHT

The most typical directional problem in terms of pitching are shots pulled left of the target. It happens because the player swings the club down too abruptly from the top, pulling the clubhead across the ball on a sharp outside-in swing path. This happens a lot when there's pressure on the shot and anxiety causes a too-quick downswing. Beware, however, that trying to slow the swing down may result in *deceleration,* when you fight the natural force of gravity on the clubhead in an attempt to steer it and keep the swing slow and smooth. Instead, your goal should be to let the clubhead peak slowly at the top of the backswing, make a smooth change of direction into the downswing, and then accelerate the clubhead through impact.

To help you make an even, rhythmic motion imagine a roller coaster as it accelerates through the bottom of a large dip in the tracks or a child on a swing, swinging back, coming to a slow stop at the peak, then swinging down, accelerating toward the ground.

THE CUT LOB

The *cut lob* is a variation on the standard pitch shot that allows you to hit the ball on an even higher, sharper-arcing trajectory than a normal wedge shot.

It's a great weapon to have when you're within pitching distance of the pin but you have very little green to work with and a hazard between you and the target forces you to carry the ball to the hole. Here you have a choice: Play a normal pitch, which

To encourage a smooth, accelerating downswing, imagine a chain of roller-coaster cars negotiating a large dip in the tracks.

will land the ball beyond the hole and leave a lengthy putt; or risk trying to drop the ball close with a high-flying, soft-landing lob.

MECHANICS: CUT LOB

The key to playing a cut lob is to open the face of the wedge wide at address and keep it open through impact. Opening the clubface increases the loft of the club and flattens the blade, allowing it to slide cleanly under the ball at impact, neatly cutting it from the turf the same way the sharp edge of a spatula slides under a pancake. To enhance the "knifing" action of the blade, assume an open stance and pick the club up sharply with the hands and arms. Pull the club down firmly with the left arm while staying behind the ball, and let the clubhead pass the hands by letting the left wrist cup slightly through impact. Keep the right hand from rolling over the left so the clubface points skyward after impact.

You should know that a cut shot with a wedge isn't a particularly easy play, and that there are risks involved.

First of all, there is extremely little margin for error. There isn't much room under the ball for the blade to slide under, and if you hit the shot a little thin or fat, the result will be disastrous —either a low, hard line drive or a short chili dip. Neither is desirable, especially if you're trying to negotiate a hazard. The type of lie you have should dictate whether or not you try a cut lob. The tighter the lie, the less room you have to slide the club underneath the ball. That's why it's easier to play this type of shot when the ball is sitting up in light rough than it is from a good lie in the fairway, and why it's nearly impossible to cut the ball off hardpan. Be aware, however, that if the ball is sitting up too high that it's possible to slide the blade completely under the ball without the clubface making contact!

Secondly, determining distance is tricky, especially if you don't practice playing this kind of shot often. When the landing area is very small, it's easy to leave the shot short, even when you make a good club-to-ball contact. If you decide to swing harder to make sure you stay out of trouble, you may carry the ball well past the flag, in which case you could have assumed less risk in the first place by playing a normal pitch shot.

GET MORE BACKSPIN

Being able to put backspin on a pitch shot will give you more control over the shot because it will stop faster after landing. Nearly all casual players are enamored with the way the pros are often able to land a ball on the green and make it back up, or "suck back." However, not only does it look good, but being able to stop the ball on the green is a valuable tool because it will help you keep the ball on the putting surface rather than sending it scooting off the back. Backspin, besides making a shot "pull up" upon landing, will also help approach shots and pitches hold the green by producing a high-flying, soft-landing trajectory. The more backspin you put on the ball, the higher the shot will fly and the steeper it will land, so it will roll less after touching down. This is helpful on a pitch because it allows you to fire at the flag while worrying less about how the ball will bounce and roll after landing. If for some reason there are factors present that prevent you from putting as much backspin on the ball as you normally would, such as a lie in the rough, the result will be a "flyer," which has less spin, flies lower and farther than usual, and lands "hot" with little stopping power, usually skipping well forward. A flyer that lands on the green may bounce over or roll to the back.

Backspin is a product of several components. The most important is clean club-to-ball contact. Anything intruding between the clubface and the ball will prevent the grooves of the clubface from putting much spin on the ball. That's why a shot hit from the rough won't have much bite when it lands—some of the tall blades of grass will be trapped between the ball and the clubface, cutting down on spin. Likewise, if the grain of the fairway grass is growing against you, you'll also get less backspin, because the leading edge of the club will scrape some of the blades of grass up between the ball and the face. However, if the grass is growing away from you (toward the target), you'll be able to get the club on the ball cleanly.

Grass isn't the only thing that can come between the ball and the clubface, cutting backspin and causing a flyer. Water can have the same effect, so if conditions are wet, plan on less bite and slightly lower, longer shots. This is what pros mean when they say a shot "squirted" off the clubface.

Another factor that determines the amount of backspin put on a given shot is the downswing angle. High-lofted clubs—the wedges, 9- and 8-irons—have short shafts, and thus approach the ball on a steeper downswing angle than the other clubs. The steeper the downswing angle, the more bite you'll be able to impart. That's why it's easier to make a wedge shot back up than a 3-iron shot.

The force of the downswing also plays a part in creating backspin. The harder you swing the club down, the more spin you'll get. That's why powerful players like Greg Norman and Craig Stadler can really make the ball "dance." It's also the reason why you'll often see a player, when playing a par five that can't be reached in two shots, leave his second shot purposely far enough short of the green so he can hit a full wedge in. That will allow him to hit the ball with a full swing, so he can put maximum bite on the shot to stop the ball on the green. This is common when the greens are very fast, such as at the U.S. Open.

The direction of the wind also plays a part in backspin. You'll get more spin hitting directly into the wind, less with the wind behind you. That's why it's tough to stop a shot quickly with a breeze at your back.

Remember, however, that even if the lie, club selection and wind allow you to put a lot of backspin on the shot, how quickly

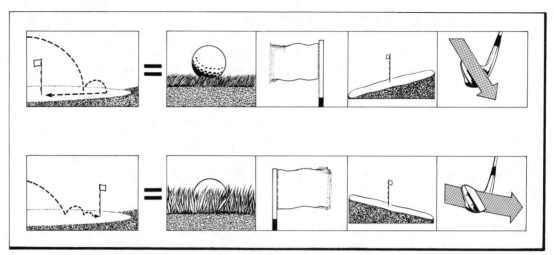

Factors that increase the chances of making the ball "suck back" (top, l–r): a clean lie, grass growing toward the target, a headwind, the green sloping against you, and a descending downswing path. Factors that are unfavorable for making the ball stop quickly (bottom, l–r): a shaggy lie, a tailwind, the green sloping away from you, and a shallow downswing path.

it stops and/or backs up also depends heavily on the character of the putting surface. You'll get more bite on a soft, well-watered green than a hard, dry one. Also, where you land the ball has to be either level or sloping back toward you in order to make the ball jerk back. No golfer can make a golf ball spin backward up a hill.

Despite all of this information, many players probably still aren't going to have much luck getting enough backspin to make the ball stop quickly. The stumbling block is that they aren't making clean enough contact. From a lie in the fairway, you don't have to strike the ball precisely in order to produce a satisfactory shot. In order to get maximum backspin, you've got to put the clubface on the ball as fully and cleanly as possible to experience a "click" at impact with the ball jumping off the club. The best way to practice this kind of perfect contact is to hit shots off very firm hardpan, or off asphalt with an old wedge. To get a decent result from a surface this firm, you can't err with your contact: Either you get the clubface on the ball cleanly, or you get a lousy result.

THE BUMP AND RUN

You don't always have to loft the ball to the green when you're within pitching distance. Sometimes conditions warrant what's known as a *bump-and-run* shot—a low shot that bounces well short of the target and rolls to its destination. This type of shot is common in the United Kingdom, where conditions on the seaside links are generally windy, wreaking havoc with high, soft wedge shots. Also, U.K. courses are generally firmer, making it harder to stop a high-flying pitch. Not so here in the United States, where most courses are well-watered and playing conditions are soft, making high, steep-landing shots the best way to attack the flag.

However, you will occasionally run into circumstances when a bump and run will be your best option for getting the ball close. Here are a few examples of when this kind of shot may prove to be a smart play:

- When the wind is severe. Your home course may not be seaside, but every so often a very strong inland wind can kick up and make it tough to play a high pitch.
- When the putting surface slopes sharply away from you, making it impossible to keep a high shot from rolling down the hill and well away from the hole. Instead, you might

bump the ball low and let it run to the edge of the green, where it will trickle slowly down to the cup.

- When the green is elevated and you have very little putting surface between the fringe and the cup to work with. Trying to get the ball close by popping it high means dropping it into a very small landing area. The bump-and-run option is to bounce the ball into the hill and let it scoot up and over the top, then trickle down to the hole.
- When the pin is in the back of the green, giving you a lot of surface to work with, and the area is basically flat. Instead of hitting the ball high, play the shot like a very long chip.
- When the greens are hard, making it difficult to keep an incoming shot that lands on the surface from bouncing to the back or going over.
- When the green is two-tiered and the pin is cut back onto the upper portion. Instead of attempting to land the ball on the back tier with a high pitch, you can bump the ball onto the bottom tier and let it run up the ramp to the hole. If you try this, make sure the ball is down and rolling before it hits the slope; otherwise it could bounce into the hill and stop, or bounce completely over the hill and roll long.
- A bump and run is also a safe shot to play when there's pressure on. Suppose you're fifty yards from the green, and need only to get the ball on and two-putt to win the match. There's more risk of mishitting a pitch—skulling it too long or hitting it fat and leaving the ball short—than with bumping the ball low onto the green.

Depending on the conditions, it's sometimes better strategy to play a bump and run by landing the ball well short and letting it run instead of trying to loft the ball to the target.

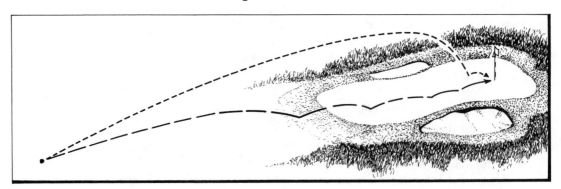

MECHANICS: BUMP AND RUN

To play a bump-and-run shot, set up in a narrow stance, either square or slightly open, with your weight on the inside of your left foot. To enhance the low, hard flight of the shot, play the ball just behind center and position your left hand slightly ahead of the ball; then let the left hand lead the clubhead through impact. The idea is not to hit down on the ball but to sweep it forward with a shallow swing, so don't crouch as much as you would to play a pitch. Keep the clubhead low to the ground on the backswing and forwardswing, and maintain a firm left wrist through impact, not allowing the toe to pass the heel until well after the ball is gone. Keep your upper body steady, but use your legs on the forwardswing, pointing your knees to the target in the follow-through.

Visualizing a Bump and Run

Playing a bump-and-run shot takes more thought than lofting a pitch. You have to read the terrain and determine how the ball will react to it, similar to the way you would read a green to see how a putt will break. Miscalculating the direction and the speed the ball will go may result in a much poorer outcome than you'd anticipated, so don't rush the shot without carefully planning it in your mind. Step back a few feet behind the ball and survey the ground ahead to determine where you want to land the ball and how hard it should be struck. Club selection should depend on both of these factors. The lower you want to play the shot, the less lofted club you should take.

Always scan for potential trouble, especially anything behind the green that a too-hard shot could roll into. If you are bumping the ball into a steep slope, be sure to hit it firmly enough to keep it from stalling and rolling back downhill.

Once you have mentally planned out the shot and picked a target area to land the ball, focus solely on that area. Forget about the green and the pin. If you calculated correctly and land the ball in the target area, it will eventually end up near the hole.

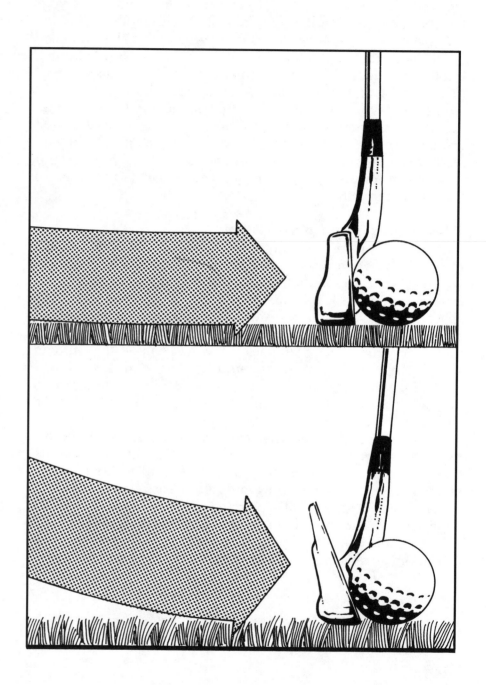

11

CHIPPING

Few things in golf are more frustrating than missing a green by only a few yards, then taking three shots to get down. (The only thing more annoying is hitting the green and three-putting.) Few amateurs recognize that being sharp on and around the greens is more valuable to scoring than having a good long game.

Maybe you've had the experience of playing with someone whose tee-to-green abilities closely mirror your own, but who outscores you with his ability to get up and down around the greens. In fact, your opponent may be *less* skilled from tee to green but still beats you because he's more adept at the short shots.

Because they need to score pars and birdies to make a living, not bogeys, there isn't a tour pro who doesn't recognize the importance of a sharp short game. Even the best ball-striker out there is going to miss a green here and there (statistics show that the average tour pro hits ten out of eighteen greens per round), and he'd better be able to make a good run at saving par when he does.

Having a good short game is also a psychological boost because you know if you should miss a green, you have confidence in your ability to save par. That takes some heat off your approach shots. Also, being able to hit the ball close from just off the green obviously leaves you with a short putt, which takes some pressure off your putting.

Finally, a good short game allows you not only to salvage a decent score on days when your tee-to-green game isn't quite up to snuff, but also to keep a good round going if you miss a green. Any player knows that it's a big letdown when, in the midst of a good round, you miss a green, then hit a poor chip and make bogey. On the contrary, if you hit a good chip and save par in the same situation, you get a psychological lift.

MECHANICS: THE CHIPPING STROKE

Styles vary in chipping; there is no right or wrong way to do it. Some players like to use a lot of wrist action, while others prefer more of an arm-and-shoulder motion. Whichever you prefer, it's usually best to make your chipping stroke similar to your putting stroke, since a chip is basically an extension of a putt. However you choose to do it, there are certain fundamentals that should be part of every chipping stroke in order to insure both consistency and accuracy.

First, your stance should be narrow, yet balanced with your weight shaded toward the inside of the left foot. It's best to stand slightly open to give yourself a better view of the target and target line.

Second, be sure to set the clubface at the proper angle by

When chipping, assume a narrow, slightly open stance with your left hand just ahead of the ball, which is played opposite the left heel.

The chipping stroke should be similar to your putting stroke. This player uses an arm-and-shoulder motion with little body movement.

Don't allow the clubhead to pass the left hand until after impact.

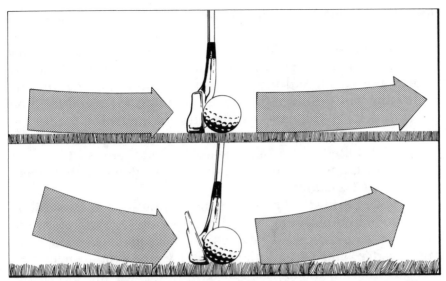

Although your chipping stroke should resemble your putting stroke, you need to make a slightly more descending downswing when chipping (bottom) than when putting (top).

playing the ball opposite your left heel and making sure that your left hand is just ahead of the ball. When you hit the shot, make a rhythmic motion, not allowing the clubhead to pass the left hand before impact nor letting the left hand get ahead of the clubhead. Also, when making the stroke, keep your body still and strive to put the clubface cleanly on the ball, since mishitting the shot fat or thin causes more poor results than bad direction to the left or right.

Keep the club low to the ground on the backswing and forwardswing to put as little backspin on the ball as possible. The slight backspin that is imparted should be "killed" on the first bounce so the ball rolls freely after that.

Keep the clubface moving straight toward the target through impact without letting the toe pass the heel; otherwise you'll impart hookspin on the ball that will make it bounce to the left when it lands.

THE ANATOMY OF A CHIP

The strategy behind chipping is simple: Land the ball safely on the putting surface as soon as possible so it can run like a putt. Therefore, your landing area will always be just inside the fringe. Lower-lofted clubs, like the 4-, 5- and 6-irons will hit lower, harder chips that roll a long way after landing. Higher-lofted clubs, like the 9-iron, pitching wedge and sand wedge, will pop the ball up higher so it lands softer and doesn't roll as far upon landing.

Club selection should depend on the distance the ball lies from the edge of the green, the distance the pin is cut from the edge of the green, and the speed of the surface. Generally, the farther the ball lies from the green, the more loft you'll need on the club to carry the ball over the edge of the fringe, yet land it softly enough so that it doesn't skip across the green and roll too far. A high-lofted club is also needed when there is little green to work with and you need to flop the ball down with a steep, soft-landing trajectory.

Besides getting the ball down and rolling as soon as possible, the idea behind chipping with different clubs is to allow you to make the same basic stroke every time. Instead of using one club, say a wedge, and varying the force of your swing to make the ball go different distances, you simply change the loft of the club, keeping the length and force of the swing about the same. That way, once you've examined the situation, chosen your club and a landing area, it's left to you only to aim the ball and hit it solidly to your landing area. The rest is automatic.

PLANNING THE SHOT

When it comes to playing a chip, you have to determine your *landing area*—where you want the ball to land—and *finishing area*—where you want the ball to finish.

As mentioned earlier, your landing area should usually be on the green, a few feet past the edge of the fringe. Carry the ball over the frog hair by a comfortable margin, since landing the ball in it can cause it to kick left or right, or take some of the steam off the shot. When choosing a landing area, remember that it won't always be directly on the target line. If the surface slopes to the right or left, you have to plan for it by aiming away from the cup and letting the slope bring the ball back to it, just as you would allow for the break when stroking a putt.

Your finishing area should be within three or four feet of the hole, on the low side, leaving yourself an uphill putt. This is especially important if the green is extremely fast or the hole is cut on a severe slope, because you will want to leave yourself the easiest possible putt. Under extreme conditions, you'll be better off leaving a four-footer straight uphill than a slick down-hill or sidehill-two-footer.

Occasionally the situation will require that you gamble on the unpredictability of the fringe and land the ball there in order to get it to stop near the pin. Larry Mize had to make this kind

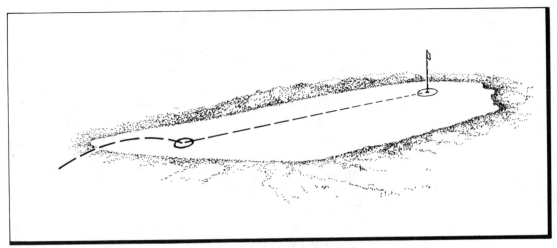

When visualizing a chip, pick out a landing area and a finishing area; then decide what club you'll need to make the shot happen.

of decision on the shot that earned him the sudden-death playoff win over Greg Norman and Seve Ballesteros in the 1987 Masters. After Ballesteros had three-putted the first extra hole (number 10 at Augusta) to drop out of the playoff, Mize and Norman proceeded to the 11th, a 455-yard par four with a large pond closely guarding the front of the green. Both players drove in the fairway, and then Mize, playing first, pushed his approach well right of the green. Norman followed with a safe shot to the right side of the green, which stopped on the fringe about 35 feet from the flag. Now Mize faced an extremely difficult shot: a long chip to a green as slick as glass that also sloped away from him. His ball lay slightly below the putting surface on an upslope, but the lie was good. He lay about 30 feet from the edge of the green, with another 70 feet of green to the cup. After sizing up the situation and visualizing the possibilities, he realized that if he landed the ball on the green, even using a lofted club, the shot would be too hot and the ball would run well past the hole. With Norman in two-putt distance, he needed to get the ball close. In his favor was the fact that earlier in the day when playing the 11th, he had faced a 20-foot putt for par along the same line and made it, so he knew what kind of line the ball would take once he got it down and rolling. The trick was to keep it from landing too hard, and the only way to do that was drop it in the fringe. The shot came off as planned, the ball landing in the fringe and bouncing forward on the line that Mize had intended. Even so, it was moving quickly when it got to the hole, but it hit the pin squarely and dropped in for an incredible birdie three. Stunned, Norman missed his long bid to tie, and Mize had won the Masters.

GOING FOR IT

A chip isn't necessarily a defensive shot. There will be times when conditions are favorable for you to try to sink a chip rather than just try to get it close. Whether you go for it or not should depend on the situation. If the green is fairly flat and you're within 40 feet of the pin or less, by all means try to sink it. With the ball laying off the green, you have the advantage of leaving the pin in. Many golfers mistakenly believe that leaving the pin in is detrimental because it prevents some shots from going in. This isn't the case. If the ball bounces off the stick and doesn't go in, it means it was hit too hard, pin or no pin. In many instances, the pin will stop a ball that's running too fast so it drops in or finishes near the hole.

Be realistic when deciding whether to go for it. For the most part, if there's a lot of break involved, or a big downhill slope, play it smart and concentrate on trying to get the ball near the cup. But if conditions are favorable, be sure to visualize the ball going in. Most amateurs are content to imagine a chip finishing near the hole. That's fine, but if you sense that you're in a position to actually sink the shot, be sure to complete your mental picture by seeing the ball drop.

TO CHIP OR NOT TO CHIP?

Sometimes it's hard to decide whether to chip a ball that lies just off the green or to putt it. Usually, your best bet is to use your putter whenever you can, mainly because it's harder to mishit a putt than a chip. In most cases a poorly hit putt will work out as well, if not better, than a good chip.

Your decision whether to chip or putt should depend mainly on the fringe—how much you have to negotiate and how high it is. If the grass between the ball and the green is cut low, you can putt from as much as ten or fifteen feet off the green. If, however, the fringe grass is high, you may want to chip it even from only a couple feet off the surface.

FRINGE BENEFITS

Once in a while your ball will come to rest on the fringe right up against the collar. The ball is sitting down snugly on the fringe, but the grass behind it is higher, making it tough to get a clubface

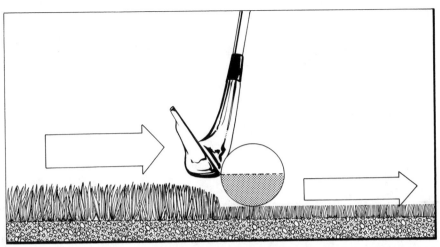

When trying to belly the ball intentionally from the edge of the fringe, keep the clubhead moving level to the ground and be sure to make contact at or slightly above the ball's equator.

cleanly on the back of the ball. There are a couple of choices here.

One is to roll the ball by intentionally bellying it with the leading edge of a sand wedge. This works because the large, flat flange will glide through the higher grass instead of getting caught in it. The tricky part is making sure that you strike the ball either at or above the equator in order to get it rolling. If you make contact below the equator, you risk popping the ball weakly in the air and leaving it well short. In the same vein, be careful not to cheat too high above the equator or you'll top the ball weakly, again leaving it short. Keep the clubhead moving as level as possible—don't chop down on the ball—and keep the club moving forward in the follow-through, as you would when putting.

Since there isn't much margin for error here, it's a good idea to practice this shot before trying it on the course.

Another option is to take a wedge and play the ball slightly farther back in your stance than usual with your hands ahead. Pick up the club abruptly by hinging your wrists, then drop the clubhead almost straight down on the back of the ball. This technique allows you to avoid swinging the clubhead through the high grass, but be prepared that the ball will move low and hard. Should you decide to take this approach, take extreme care to make precise contact: If you hit the ball only slightly fat, it will barely move; while hitting it just a little thin will cause it to scoot well past the target.

12

GREENSIDE SAND

If you're an experienced player, you've probably heard or read a thousand times that the explosion shot from sand is the "simplest shot in golf, because you don't have to put the clubface on the ball to get out of the hazard." Exactly *why* this shot is so "simple" isn't clear, since scores of golfers still fear the greenside bunker shot more than any other in golf. Usually they are defeated before they ever step into the bunker, based on their many poor past experiences. The worst fear a bad sand player has is that he'll leave the ball in the trap and have to hit the nightmare shot again. The second worst fear is that he'll hit the ball too cleanly, knocking it clear over the green and possibly into more trouble. The truth is, sand is *less* hazardous than you think if you know how to play out of it and have confidence in your ability to do so. During the third round of the 1986 U.S. Open at Shinnecock Hills, Raymond Floyd pushed his drive on the 15th hole into long rough to the right. Fifteen at Shinnecock is a short part four, so Floyd knew he could slash a short-iron out and land the ball on the green, but he worried that because the high grass wouldn't allow him to get any backspin on the shot, the ball would roll off the back of the green, leaving a very difficult chip from the heavy greenside rough. After studying the situation, Floyd formulated an unusual strategy: Instead of trying to land the ball on the green and risk bouncing over, he decided to aim intentionally for a greenside sand trap in front. Floyd's reasoning was that, being an excellent sand player, he would have a better chance of getting up and down from the bunker than he would from the greenside rough. After successfully putting his approach in the trap, Floyd's ensuing explosion rolled into the hole for a birdie three. He went on to win the tournament.

THE EXPLOSION EXAMINED

Understanding the explosion shot and being able to picture what's happening in the cloud of sand that erupts at impact is critical to overcoming your fear and learning to play the shot correctly.

Take a moment and recollect the first time you attempted a shot from greenside sand, if you can. If you had no previous instruction or advice, you probably tried to pick the ball cleanly off the sand. If this was the case, you may have discovered what happens if you unintentionally trap some sand between the clubface and ball: The sand acted as a cushion, deadening impact and causing the ball to fly much shorter than you'd anticipated—probably remaining in the bunker.

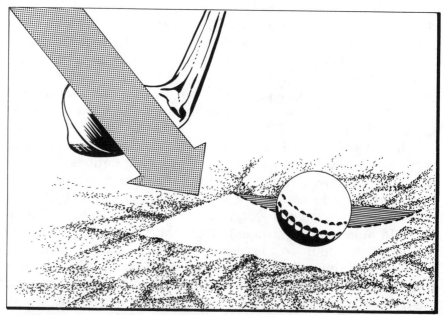

The idea behind the explosion shot is that if you displace the sand that the ball rests on, the ball will go with it.

Trying to pick the ball cleanly off the surface without taking any sand is a difficult task. Usually you end up either getting some sand or not getting enough of the ball. Instead, it's better to anticipate the deadening effect of the sand on impact and intentionally hit the sand behind the ball with the clubhead, making a forceful swing to drive the sand—and the ball with it —out of the trap and onto the green.

What you are actually doing is displacing a small section of sand with the clubhead. The ball just happens to rest on top of that bit of sand, so when the sand flies, the ball goes with it. The reason the explosion isn't as hard as it may appear is that there is such a large margin for error in the area where the clubface makes contact with the sand. Whether you hit one, two, three or even four inches behind the ball, you still should be able to get the ball out of the trap and onto the green if you've made a brisk enough downswing.

MECHANICS OF AN EXPLOSION

To play an explosion shot, set up open and dig your feet in just deep enough to stabilize yourself. Don't focus on the ball; instead pick a small mark two or three inches behind the ball and address that, playing it opposite the center of your stance. If you can, focus on something that physically stands out, like a dark grain of sand. Open the clubface wide so it faces the sky and hover it lightly just above the surface, keeping your hands and wrists loose, not tight.

To play an explosion, first open the clubface and set up in an open stance, digging your feet in just enough for stability.

Make an abrupt, upright backswing by cocking the wrists quickly so the clubshaft points nearly straight up.

Keep the clubhead moving so it clears the sand, and keep your head down until the clubhead has passed your left hip.

The clubface should point to the sky in the follow-through, indicating that you've kept the right hand from rolling over the left through impact.

Pick the club up abruptly with your arms and a quick cock of the left wrist, so the shaft points almost straight up. (Use the image of the shaft pointing straight to the sky if you have trouble swinging back on an abrupt plane). Keeping your eye on the spot you've picked in the sand and your upper body quiet, pull the club down firmly with the left hand, accelerating the clubhead into the sand and bouncing it through. Do not allow the right hand to roll over the left—the clubface should face the sky in the follow-through—and keep your head down until the clubhead has passed your left hip. When you finally look up the ball should be on the green, hopefully close.

HOW A SAND WEDGE WORKS

The head of a sand wedge is designed to make an explosion shot easier. The flange is especially large and rounded, enhancing its ability to bounce upward and clear of the sand instead of digging down into it. That's what allows you to hit down briskly into the sand behind the ball without fear that the clubhead will get mired. The more you open the clubface, the more "bounce" you'll get.

The large, rounded flange of a sand wedge is designed to bounce upward and out of the sand instead of digging down and stalling.

All golfers owe their thanks for the sand wedge to one of the game's greatest players, Gene Sarazen, who invented the first one. Before that, the explosion was one of the hardest, most unpredictable shots in golf because the blade of the wedge tended to cut downward into the sand, often getting bogged down and stuck. Sarazen realized that a large, rounded flange would bounce upward and out of the sand instead of digging downward. So he experimented with enlarging the flange by applying solder to the head of a normal wedge, and tried explosion after explosion until he was satisfied. And, fortunately for every player then and now, the rest is history.

CONQUERING YOUR FEAR

Playing an explosion shot sounds pretty simple—and it is—but many poor bunker players claim that although they understand what happens during an explosion, they still have problems with playing it. Here are a few common mistakes that prevail, and how to cure them.

Deceleration

Probably the one fault that results in more poor explosion shots than any other is deceleration. Past disasters cause the player to be tentative, and a cautious downswing will spoil any shot, whether it's a drive, a chip or a putt. It's crucial that the downswing be aggressive on an explosion shot in order to create enough pressure to carry the ball out of the hazard despite the deadening effect of the sand. To make up for the cushioning of the sand, you have to swing approximately twice as hard as you would if the ball were sitting cleanly on short grass. You must trust that striking the sand behind the ball will effectively minimize the force of the downswing and the "spring" of the ball off the clubface so that the ball will fly shorter than usual.

To prevent a timid downswing, before the shot visualize striking the sand hard enough to send a shower of it over the lip. Keep that vision in mind and make it happen, making sure to follow through with the clubhead. If you strike behind the ball and throw the sand beneath it over the lip, the ball is sure to clear the lip as well.

Poor Impact Point

Poor impact point occurs when the clubhead doesn't enter the sand where the player intended, striking either too close to the ball or too far behind it. If you hit too close to the ball, you'll take only a pinch of sand or accidentally pick the ball clean. Either way, the ball sails much farther than intended.

The opposite happens when the club strikes too far behind the ball, taking too much sand. The clubhead gets bogged down in all that sand and the ball falls short of the target.

Missing your intended impact point with the clubhead usually happens when anxiety over the shot results in head and body movement during the downswing. Bear in mind that the spine is the center of the swing; any upper-body movement that shifts the position of the spine will also shift your swing arc, greatly minimizing the chances that the clubhead will return to the proper impact point.

Lifting the head causes the spine to lift upward as well, shifting the arc with it and causing you to take little or no sand.

Another common mistake is dropping the right shoulder, which can happen when a golfer tries to swing too hard. The spine lowers slightly on the downswing, shifting the swing arc down with it so the club digs into the sand too far behind the ball.

Eliminate extraneous motion that can result in poor impact point by remembering that, although you've made a few minor adjustments, the swing motion is still the same. On the downswing, your attention should be focused on the mark you've chosen in the sand, your weight should be on your left side, your shoulders should rotate smoothly around your spine, and your head should stay behind the ball until after impact.

REGULATING DISTANCE

There are a few ways to regulate the length of an explosion shot. The simplest is to hit the same distance behind the ball every time while varying the force of the downswing.

A more sophisticated way to control distance is to vary how far you hit behind the ball, taking less sand for longer shots, more sand for shorter shots. This method, although popular with the pros, is not recommended for the average amateur, who doesn't practice enough to be very precise about clubhead entry point.

Your best bet is to gauge your swing force to determine distance. However, there are some additional adjustments you can make that will be helpful on extremely long or extremely short explosions.

Long Explosions

One of the most difficult shots in golf is the long explosion, because it's hard to be distance accurate. If you have to blast the ball twenty yards or longer, square the clubface up and assume only a slightly open stance; then make a flatter, more shallow backswing and downswing. The combination of the square face and shallow swing will result in a lower, harder trajectory, making the ball go farther than usual.

Short Explosions

Very short explosions can be tricky too, but certain adjustments can make them easier. Start by opening the clubface very wide and flat, so it points to the sky. Next, pick the club up very quickly with your hands, making a very abrupt, upright backswing and downswing. Hit down aggressively, even though the target is only a few yards away, because most of the force you generate will be expended on popping the ball almost straight up.

BURIED LIES

Greenside sand play would be easier if your lie was always good, but sometimes the ball will burrow down into the sand, making it tougher to get out. Usually it takes a combination of a high, steep-landing shot and soft sand for the ball to be buried, but if it should happen, you'd better know how to extricate it, or else it could take you two shots to get free of the trap.

A semi-buried ball is usually referred to as a "fried egg" because that's what it resembles. With this type of lie, the bottom of the ball is just slightly below the surface of the sand. Because of this, you have to dig down deeper to get the club underneath the ball to blast it free. To do this, square up the face of your sand wedge, play the ball just forward of center, hands even with the ball at address, and hit down about two inches behind the ball. Power the club down and through in order to drive it deep into the sand to prevent the leading edge of the club from bellying the ball.

If the ball is out-and-out "buried" so that more than half of it is below the surface of the sand, set up the same way but use your pitching wedge and hit only one inch behind the ball. The smaller flange and sharper leading edge will slice downward through the sand more easily. Swing hard: The sand surrounding the ball will offer a lot of resistance, and the idea is to "shock" the ball free.

Any kind of buried ball will be difficult to control, since it will fly out low and with no backspin. Consider it a good shot if you get the ball out of the bunker and safely on the putting surface. It's a tremendous shot if you get it within five feet.

CHIPPING FROM SAND

There's no rule that says you have to explode from sand—indeed, there will be some circumstances when you'll be better off trying to chip the ball out of a bunker by picking the ball cleanly. For example, if you have little sand and a very low lip to negotiate, you can opt to play the shot like a typical chip. The only difference is that you have to be very precise with your clubhead control to make sure that the clubhead strikes the ball first before hitting the sand. Only attempt this kind of play if the lie is clean and the surface is either flat or uphill.

To hit the shot, play it as you would a typical chip, incorporating these tips to increase your chances of "ball-first" contact:

Position the ball just behind center in your stance, choke down an extra inch for added clubhead control, and keep the clubhead low on the backswing. A little food for thought: If your clubhead contact errs toward the "thin" side, you'll still most likely get the ball out of the bunker and onto the green with passable results, whereas hitting "fat" will result in disaster—you'll probably leave the ball in the sand.

Because hitting the ball cleanly or not is the "make-or-break" factor of chipping from sand, the key visual image you should have is of the clubface striking the ball cleanly.

PUTTING OUT OF A BUNKER

You can also get out of a bunker by rolling the ball over the sand and out, but only if conditions specifically allow it. The lie should be clean, the surface should be smooth and firm, and there should be little or no fringe. As with chipping, making clean contact should be your highest priority. You may want to play the ball about two inches ahead of normal, so you can catch the ball more on the upswing, imparting overspin that will help make it scoot out of the sand. If you aren't comfortable playing the ball farther forward than usual, you can keep it in your normal position. Don't, however, play it back in hopes of increasing your chances of hitting the ball first: You will hit down on the ball, pushing it into the sand and perhaps causing it to get bogged down.

Don't be embarrassed to putt from a bunker if the conditions are right. It doesn't mean you're afraid of the sand; you are merely playing the highest percentage shot.

PART IV

PUTTING

13

GREENREADING

Putting is rather mysterious. In many ways it is very different from the tee-to-green game, and sometimes you'll see a player who is very proficient at ball-striking but only an average or below-average putter. Likewise, some golfers make up for a lot of shortcomings between the tee and green thanks to their talent at rolling the ball into the hole.

This kind of discrepancy has even been observed in professional players over the years. There have been a number of tour pros who were known chiefly for their ability to putt. Bobby Locke, the great professional from South Africa, wasn't particularly concerned with how he got the ball onto the green. Once it was there, however, the real game began. When Locke had the putter in hand he devoted complete concentration to getting the ball in the hole, and he had a great reputation for being able to do so.

Billy Casper was another tour pro known during his prime for his uncanny knack for putting. Ben Hogan, one of the greatest ball-strikers who ever lived but not known for his putting, once told Casper that he would be "selling hot dogs" on tour if he didn't know how to putt. Today, Casper is still sinking his share on the Senior Tour. Currently on the regular tour, Ben Crenshaw has tremendous talent with the flatstick that tends to overshadow the rest of his game.

Interestingly, some players lose their putting ability as they get older, while just as interestingly, there are many players who are able to maintain their putting prowess despite age. Besides Casper, Bob Charles, the pro from New Zealand and one of the top players today on the U.S. Senior Tour, has been known throughout his career for his fine stroke and is still making everything in sight.

Others have struggled with the blade on and off throughout their careers, seesawing between bouts of success and serious problems. Sam Snead was known not only for his wonderful golf swing, but also for his struggles on the greens. These days, Bernhard Langer of Germany is famous for his off-again, on-again relationship with the putter.

Most amateurs have plenty of room for improvement in their putting games, either by learning to make and practicing a consistent stroke, or by thinking their way around the greens more efficiently. Never underestimate the importance of a good putting game, since the putter is almost always the club you'll hit the most shots with in a given round.

WHAT IS PUTTING?

When you think of putting in simple terms, it doesn't seem very difficult. You determine what direction and how hard you want the ball to go, then hit it so it rolls in that direction and at that speed. The target is more accessible than ever—instead of being tens of yards away, it is tens of feet or less. Yet golfers often complicate putting, worrying over it so that it becomes much harder than it should be. If you've ever noticed, kids are usually good at putting, probably because they see it as the fairly simple thing it is without getting caught up in thinking too much. But sometimes the more you play, the more you think about putting (especially when you have a bad streak of it), which can be detrimental. Remember, your goal is to plan, visualize and react to the ball, and a putt should be no different than any other kind of shot.

This isn't to say that the putting game is simple or easy. In fact, it takes a lot of intelligence and concentration to be a consistently good putter. Curtis Strange, in his book *Win and Win Again*, stated that "putting takes more guts than any other part of the game." When you take to the green with your putter in hand, it's the end of the line for that hole—you can make up for a bad drive with a good recovery shot, or a poor approach with a decent chip or pitch; but when you miss a putt, then that's a stroke gone forever.

VISUALIZATION AND PUTTING

Visualization may be more important in putting than anywhere else in golf. Why? Most golf shots are hit through the air, allowing you to negotiate any trouble between the ball and the target by carrying over it. But when putting, the irregularities in the surface—slopes, swales, dips, humps—must be negotiated head on by rolling the ball over them and allowing for their effect on the path the ball takes. That's where your ability to read the surface and imagine the effects it will have on how the ball rolls plays a huge part in your ability to putt well.

But greenreading is only half the job. As mentioned above, you must be able to hit the ball in the direction and at the speed you've determined is correct. You may be the best greenreader in the world, but if you can't hit the ball with the direction and speed you wish, you won't make many putts. Likewise, you can have a terrific stroke and excellent feel, but if you can't read greens correctly, you won't make many putts, either.

In addition, when you putt, the target you're aiming for is the smallest you'll face. Your goal isn't just to get it near the cup, but into it, which means you're trying to hit something 4.25 inches wide. To be a good putter, you've got to be exacting in order to hit a target that small consistently.

SEEING THE LINE

After a good putting round, you'll often hear a tour pro talk about how clearly he could "see the line." What he means is how well he was able to imagine the line that the ball would take to the hole. "Seeing the line" wouldn't be very difficult if every green was perfectly flat—all you'd have to do would be to imagine a straight line running from your ball to the hole. But most greens aren't flat; instead they gently slope, roll and undulate, so to sink a putt you have to determine how the ball will react to the surface. If the green between your ball and the cup slopes from right to left, you'll have to play the ball out to the right and let it curve with the slope back down to the cup. The better your ability to judge how the slope will affect the way the ball rolls, and to formulate a picture in your mind of what the putt will look like, the better your chances of making it.

If you've ever played early in the morning when there is dew on the greens, you've seen the way a putt leaves a trail showing you the exact line the putt traveled on. That's exactly the kind of thing you should visualize before you stroke a putt; then try to roll the ball so it travels along that line.

To increase your chances of hitting a good putt, clearly visualize the line you think it will take to the hole.

To visualize the correct line, though, you must first be adept at reading the green to tell what kind of line you think the putt will take—the *break*—and how fast the putt will roll—the *speed*.

Speed

The speed of a putt depends on the character of the surface you have to negotiate, which can be influenced by several factors: The type of grass, how low it is cut, whether it is wet or dry, whether you are putting with the grain, against the grain or cross-grain, and whether you are putting uphill or downhill.

Most golf courses in the northern United States feature bent grass greens, while greens in the southern U.S. are usually seeded with Bermuda grass.

The difference is that Bermuda blades are coarser, so the *grain*—the direction the grass grows in—has an impact on the speed and line the putt will take. The finer blades of bent grass make it generally faster than Bermuda, but the grain has little effect on the speed or direction of the putt.

Never underestimate the effect of grain on Bermuda greens—taking it into account can mean the difference between making a putt and having it slide by; or between toppling it over the front edge of the cup and leaving it on the front lip. There are certain clues that will tip off the direction of the grain. Check around the edges of the hole to see if you can spot which way the blades are pointing. Look at the surface of the green: If it appears shiny, the grain is slanting away from you; if it looks dull, the grain is pointing toward you or to one side. The longer fringe grass may give you some insight into which direction it's growing. Also, grass tends to grow in the direction of water, so if there are any greenside water hazards present, look toward the water to find out the direction of the grain.

When trying to find out about the grain, use your eyes only. It's against the rules to use your putterhead or any other object to scrape the green to find out what direction the blades are growing.

If a putt is with the grain, it will move faster than a putt that's going against the grain. If the grain is toward one side, it will influence the ball to move in that direction. For example, if you have what looks like a straight ten-foot putt, but the direction of the grain is to the left, then plan for the putt to move slightly from right to left.

Whether the grass is bent or Bermuda, slope is obviously something that will always affect speed. That's why it's always a good idea to get a side view of your putt to see if you're heading up or downhill, in case it isn't obvious. This is especially important if the green is very fast, since the slicker the surface, the more a downhill slope will magnify the speed of a putt. Likewise, an uphill slope on a slow surface will quickly sap a putt's power.

Remember that whenever you are putting straight uphill, you can afford to hit the ball a little firmer than usual. That's because the angle of the slope causes the back of the cup to be higher than the front, so it acts something like a backstop, creating less chance for a firm putt to jump over the back lip. Another reason to be aggressive when heading uphill is that if you miss, the slope will slow the ball quickly, leaving you a short comeback putt. (One of the cardinal sins in golf is to leave an uphill putt with little or no break short of the hole.)

Conversely, a slippery downhill putt is made even more difficult by the combination of the slope making the putt roll faster with the back of the cup slightly lower than the front, so a putt rolling fast has more of a chance of jumping completely over the hole. And, of course, the hill will make a missed putt roll even farther past than usual.

The height of the grass also directly influences speed. The shorter the grass, the faster the surface, so a green will be fastest immediately after it has been cut in the morning and grow slower toward late afternoon.

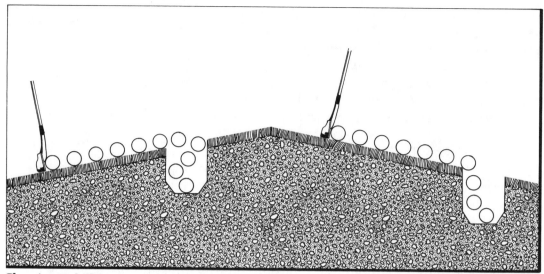

Charging Uphill Putt   **Dying Downhill Putt**

Be aggressive and charge the cup when putting uphill (left) because the back lip is higher than the front; conversely, your strategy going downhill should be to topple the ball over the front lip since the back of the cup is lower than the front.

Another thing that will slow the speed of a green down later in the day is moisture. If you are playing at dusk, as the sun goes down and dew forms on the grass, it will slow the ball as it rolls. Of course, any other form of moisture on the surface of the green, such as rain or water from a sprinkler, will also slow a putt down.

Break

Your first task in determining the break should be simply to step back about five or six feet behind the ball and survey the ground that lies between it and the cup. How much it deviates from level, or slants, plays a big part in how much the ball will break, or curve. The more the ground slopes, the more the putt will break.

Check carefully to see if the ground appears to slope to the left, to the right, or seems relatively flat. Look at the cup itself—does it seem to slant slightly one way or the other? Examine the character of the landscape toward the back of the green from where you're standing—does it appear to slope in a particular direction? If you poured a bucket of water on your line, which way do you think it would flow?

Another way to determine the direction that the ground on

which you're standing slopes is to *plumb bob* with your putter. To plumb bob, position yourself about five feet behind the ball so that the cup, the ball and your dominant eye form a straight line. Stand up straight, with your feet about shoulder-width, and dangle your putter lightly between your fingers by the end of the grip so the shaft hangs freely, straight down (certain styles of putters with the head offset from the shaft will not work because they won't hang straight). Close your nondominant eye and position the shaft so it covers the cup. Without moving your head or any other part of your body, shift your glance to the cup—if it appears to the left of the shaft, the ground slopes from right to left. If it appears to the right of the shaft, the ground slopes from left to right. How much space between the cup and shaft is an indication of how much slope. If the cup appears behind the shaft, the ground is flat. A word of warning: Plumb-bobbing will only tell you what direction the ground that you're standing on slopes. It's very possible, especially on long putts, that the ground around the cup could slope in the opposite direction, resulting in a double-break. If you want to check the slope behind the cup, stand behind the cup and plumb bob again, this time covering the cup with the shaft and checking where the ball appears in relation to the shaft.

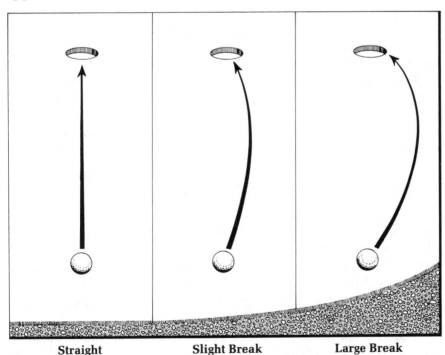

Straight   **Slight Break**   **Large Break**

Check carefully to see which way, if any, the ground slopes, since it will determine which direction and how much the putt will break.

Always be alert to any clues that will tell you about the break of your putt. Pay special attention to the way the putts of your playing partners roll, since they can sometimes tell you something about your own. Even if another player's putt isn't exactly on your line, if it is approaching the cup from the same general direction, it may tell you the direction yours will break. If it does happen to be on your line, don't miss a chance to "go to school" by watching it. Not only will it show you which way your putt will break, it will also give you a vivid image to replay in your head when it comes to visualizing your own.

Watch carefully, too, if another player is on your line, but on the opposite side of the cup. It's possible that the line of that putt could tell you something about how yours will break; however, there's no guarantee.

If you chip onto the green, be sure to keep an eye on how the ball breaks as it approaches or goes past the hole—another advantage to getting the ball down and rolling as quickly as possible when chipping. Likewise, if you miss a putt and it goes by the hole, don't look away in disgust (a likely reaction if the ball rolls well past), but keep watching it to find out the line you'll need for the comeback putt. Any player who prefers to charge his putts to the back of the cup can't afford *not* to do this.

Take the Side Door

Understand that when there's break involved, the ball will drop into the side of the cup in relation to where your balls lies, not over the front edge. The reason many amateurs miss breaking putts on the "low" side of the hole is because they don't visualize the ball falling in the side door, and thus don't plan for enough break.

PUTTING STRATEGY

How much a putt will break depends upon the speed of the surface and how hard you hit it. Given the same degree of slope, a putt will break less on a slower green than a faster green, less if you hit it harder than if you hit it softer. So when reading the green and visualizing the line, you have to determine how fast you intend to roll the ball.

When it comes to the speed you intend to roll the ball, there are basically two strategies: *charging the cup*, so the ball hits the back lip and drops; or *toppling* the ball in, so that its momentum carries just far enough to reach the hole and topple over the edge.

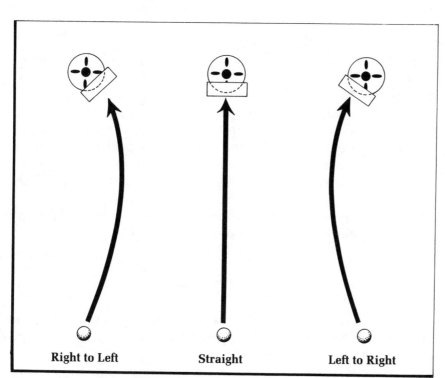

| Right to Left | Straight | Left to Right |

On breaking putts, plan for the ball to drop in the "side door."

The firmer you stroke the ball, the less it will break.

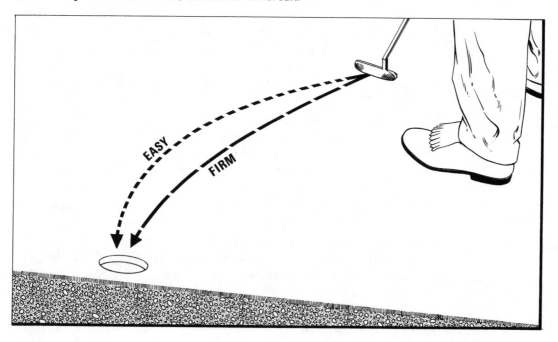

Toppling

Most players prefer to topple the ball into the hole because you have to be less precise with the line. Even if the ball doesn't roll directly at the center of the cup, it can still catch an edge and fall in. This way you are effectively increasing the size of the target instead of just zeroing in on the center. Conversely, if you charge the cup and don't hit the center of the back edge, chances are good that the putt will lip out. However, you have to be more conscious of speed, because for a putt to drop by grabbing just part of the cup, it *has* to be rolling very slowly when it gets there. Another advantage of toppling is that if the putt doesn't go in, you should be left with only a short tap-in.

Charging

Charging has advantages of its own, however. You can stroke the ball more aggressively, which some players feel more comfortable doing, and you can play less break, allowing you to aim more directly at the hole. You'll rarely leave a putt short of the hole (anyone who's ever rolled a crucial putt at the heart of the cup, but left it a half inch short will appreciate this). The disadvantages are, for one, a smaller target, since you now must either hit the back of the cup or lip the ball out. Another is the possibility that the ball will run past if you miss, leaving a nerve-racking comeback putt instead of a simple tap-in. To be a charge-type putter, you've got to have a lot of confidence in your ability to convert short putts. Arnold Palmer, perhaps the most famous charger in history, noted that part of the reason he went for the cup so boldly during the height of his career was because he was so sure of his ability to sink the putt coming back if he should miss, even if it was four or five feet long.

Which strategy you choose, charging or toppling, should depend on what you feel comfortable doing. However, bear in mind that certain types of putts strongly dictate one strategy over the other. For example, when faced with a putt straight uphill, even players who prefer to topple their putts should always charge it firmly for the back of the cup. Likewise, if a putt is downhill on a slick surface, the best bet is to be careful with the speed and try to topple it in, even if you are normally a charger.

There will be times when you'll want to change strategies, not just for one particular putt, but for the rest of the day. Occasionally you'll find yourself in the midst of a round when you just can't seem to get the ball to the hole. Instead, everything comes up short. Although the adage "never up, never in" is an old one, it is no less true: No matter how well you've read the green and judged the line, if you don't hit the ball hard enough to get to the hole, it has no chance of going in. If you find you've left three or four makable putts in a row short of the hole, change your tack and go for the back of the cup. It might make a difference. Likewise, if you normally charge the cup but find that you happen to be missing more comebackers than usual, tone down your attack and try to topple the ball in. Even if you don't sink the initial putt, you should at least leave the ball close enough for an easy tap-in instead of another three-putt.

THE STROKE

Earlier it was mentioned that there are two parts to putting: determining the direction and speed of a putt, and then hitting it in that direction and at that speed. To perform the second part, you've got to have a putting stroke that's mechanically sound. Effective putting strokes vary from player to player, just as good golf swings do. But there are certain common denominators that all good putters share—five of them, to be exact.

Number 1: A Comfortable, Balanced Setup with the Shoulders Square to the Line.

As long as your address position includes these three elements, you can vary any other part of it. Posture, for example: Raymond Floyd stands relatively tall with his putter, while Paul Azinger crouches low. Whichever you prefer is okay, so long as you feel comfortable and balanced—not teetering in any particular direction. This is especially important when playing in strong wind.

No matter what type of posture you favor, be sure that your shoulders are square to the line you want the ball to start rolling on. It's all right to set up with the feet and hips open, as many players like to do, but not the shoulders. (If the shoulders are also open, you'll swing the putter forward on an outside-in swing path and pull the putt left of target, unless some kind of compensation is made with the arms to coerce the clubhead onto a straight path; but doing so will interfere with the true swinging action of the club.) This is why it's important to monitor your putting alignment frequently. If you experience a sudden streak where you seem to be missing everything to the left, it could be that you're accidentally setting up with your shoulders open. It's an easy mistake to make, since you have to swivel your head to the left when taking aim in order to look from the ball to the target, possibly letting your shoulders slide open slightly.

Number 2: Eyes over the Target Line, but Not Ahead of the Ball.

Aiming a putt would be a lot easier if you could stand behind it instead of to the side, where it's more difficult to tell precisely whether the clubface is pointing down the intended target line. Since you have to stand to the side, it's best to set up with your eyes directly over the target line, but not ahead of the ball. A common cause of poor aim is that the eyes are not in a good position to see whether the clubface is pointing in the right di-

To find out if your eyes are over the line, address a ball, then hold another ball to the bridge of your nose and drop it. If it lands on the ball or in line behind it, your eyes are in good position.

rection. Check yours by setting up to stroke a ball, then holding a second ball up to the bridge of your nose (right between your eyes) and letting it drop straight down. If it lands on the ball you were addressing or directly behind it, your position is okay— your eyes are over the line. If not, you may have found the source of your aiming woes. If your eyes are outside the line, you'll unknowingly aim the ball to the left of your intended target line. If your eyes are inside the line, you'll aim right of the target line.

If you find that you've been setting up with your eyes in poor position in relation to the ball, adjust them until you can successfully drop a ball from the bridge of your nose so it lands on top of or just behind the ball you're addressing. Recheck your position frequently for a while to make sure you maintain it, or if you ever inexplicably start to miss putts left or right.

Number 3: Putterhead Swings Smoothly and Stays Low to the Ground.

Don't make the mistake of picking up the club abruptly on the backswing, since that will result in a steep downswing. You will pinch the ball into the ground at impact, causing it to skid and possibly squirt off line. Although the putter is nicknamed the "flatstick," it actually possesses about two degrees of loft. It's important that you apply that loft at impact in order to get the ball rolling well, so keep the putterhead low to the ground when you swing it back and through.

The swing, whether a long, flowing stroke or a short, aggressive, popping action should display a certain smoothness, especially in the transition from backswing to forwardswing. Putts that are pulled and pushed off line are often caused when the putter is jerked forward too quickly before the backswing has been completed.

Keep the putterhead moving low to the ground both back and through to put a good roll on the ball.

| Your address should be comfortable and balanced, with your shoulders square to the line you want the ball to start rolling on. | Swing the club back and through using your arms and shoulders, keeping the motion smooth and even. | The head and body should remain still and the left wrist firm through impact. |

Number 4: Left Wrist Remains Firm through Impact.

Whether or not you include some wrist action in your back-swing, you have to keep the left wrist relatively firm through impact to keep it from cupping and "breaking down" as you hit the ball, which will result in the putt rolling left of the intended target. However, don't freeze the left wrist into a completely stiff position, or else you'll lose some of your sense of feel and probably will leave the clubface open through impact, pushing the ball off to the right.

Number 5: Keep Your Body Still.

When a player complains he's putting poorly because he's "moving his head," the real problem is that his body is moving along with his head. When this happens, the entire path of the club-head is thrown out of whack, causing you to mishit the putt, pull it or push it. Think of it this way: If you stood behind a golfer making a stroke and, just before the putterhead made contact with the ball, you gave him a slight push—just enough to move his body a little—do you think he'd roll the ball precisely down the line he intended? Very doubtful, yet a great many golfers cause themselves to suffer the same effect by letting their bodies move, no matter how slightly, during the stroke. One of the great images to bring to mind when putting is the easy, unhurried swinging of a pendulum on a grandfather clock. But to swing the putter like a pendulum, you must keep the point from which it swings solidly fixed in one spot. There should be no motion other than the slight swiveling of shoulders and arms until the ball has been struck.

SHORT AND BRISK OR LONG AND SMOOTH?

Should you stroke the ball with a short, firm, popping action, or a long, flowing swing? The choice is up to you, because either can be effective. It's best to experiment with both and stick with the method that you feel most comfortable with. However, some players prefer to make a long, smooth stroke on all putts except short ones, when they switch to the shorter pop-stroke to roll the ball firmly home.

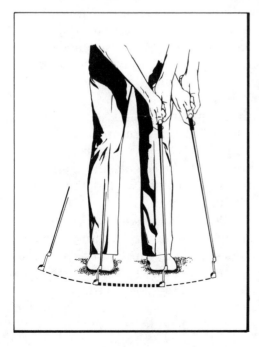

Whether you employ a long, flowing stroke or a short, popping motion depends on your personal preference.

RATING YOUR ABILITY

There is no right or wrong way to putt. If you're consistently getting the ball in the hole, you're doing it right no matter what your stroke looks like. If you aren't sinking enough putts, either your stroke needs improvement or your greenreading skills aren't up to par.

First, you've got to check your own putting statistics to find out what your putting status is. Reflect back on your last round if you can and count the number of putts you took. Ideally, "par" allows us to take two putts on every hole (36 per round), provided that every green is hit in regulation. That's not bad, but if that were the case, you wouldn't make any birdies. And if you occasionally missed a green, you didn't save par. What this all means is that every golfer should strive to take less than 36 putts for eighteen holes. Thirty is a good number to shoot for.

If you typically exceed 30 putts per round, you've got some work to do. If you've read the putt correctly, whether you make it or come close comes down to two things: your ability to roll the ball in the direction you desire and your ability to roll the ball the distance you desire.

DIRECTION

Since the cup is a small target, you have to be precise about direction. Obviously, if you don't hit the putt in the direction you want it to go, the chances of it going in are slim (unless you misread the line and the impact error works in your favor).

Directional problems can result because your ability to aim the putterface is faulty or because a flaw in your stroke is causing you to push or pull the putt off line.

You can test your directional ability on the green by finding a straight, level, ten-foot putt on the practice green (either directly with or against the grain if it's Bermuda grass, so there will be no influence on the break). Stroke twenty putts and keep track of how many you sink. Statistics show that the average tour pro, under the same conditions, will make it 70% of the time. You shouldn't expect to be as good as a tour pro (if you are, all the better), but you should be able to make no less than half of your attempts. If you miss more of these ten-footers than you make, it indicates a faulty stroke, since you know where you want to hit the putt, but you aren't making it go in that direction. Either you aren't aiming correctly or your swing path is bad, causing putts to be pushed or pulled off line.

IMPROVING AIM

If your aiming ability happens to be lacking, take heart, since it's one of the most common errors in the game. Even tour pros experience problems with it from time to time.

One aid to aiming the putterface correctly is to pick out a spot long the line a couple of feet in front of the ball and use it as an intermediate target. Once you have the blade aimed, forget about it, settle into a comfortable position and concentrate on making a good stroke.

"FEEL"

The ability to control the force of the stroke so the ball goes the desired distance is often referred to as "feel." If your sense of feel is good, you'll consistently be able to roll the ball to the hole without going too far past or coming up well short. The majority of three-putting that occurs from long range is not a result of poor direction, but poor distance control. The ball is on or close to being on line, but rolls too far or short, leaving a lengthy second putt.

Your goal on most long putts—approximately 35 feet and longer—should be to stop the ball close to the cup, leaving yourself an easy second putt. One of the oldest tricks in the putting book is to imagine that the hole is in the center of a circle six

To cut down on three-putting from long distance, imagine a circle six feet in diameter around the cup. If you stop the ball within the imaginary circle, you'll have no more than a three-footer left.

feet in diameter. If you get the ball to finish in that circle, you'll have three feet or less left for your next putt, greatly decreasing your chances of taking two putts. Pros will tell you that constantly having to face comeback putts longer than three feet can be very taxing mentally, and that the prospect of a simple tap-in is a heck of a lot less wearing on your nerves.

How Grip Determines Feel

How acute your feel is depends on how sensitive you are to the clubhead. Your hands play an important role here because they are your only contact with the club. Maintaining a light degree of grip pressure is important—squeezing the club tightly cuts down on the amount of feedback you get from your hands. When you throw a dart, you hold it lightly in your fingers so you can feel it in your fingertips and get maximum feedback. The same principle applies with a putter.

The way the handle of the putter feels in your hands can change from round to round. Some days your sensitivity is acute, and you feel as if you are touching the ball with your fingertips at impact. Other days you have less feel. On those days when you don't seem to be getting as much feedback from the clubhead, try holding it especially lightly.

MAKING SOLID CONTACT

Another cause of poor distance control is mishitting the ball, so the putt comes up well short. The longer the putt, the more it will hurt you to mishit the ball. In other words, if you fail to hit a ten-footer solidly, it will probably come up two or three feet short at most, still leaving a very makable putt. But if you mishit a 50-footer, you may come up short by as much as ten or 15 feet. A putt is just like any other shot in golf: You've got to hit the ball with the sweet spot to get the best results.

To find the sweet spot on your putterface, dangle the shaft straight down by holding it lightly on the end of the grip with the fingers of one hand. Tap the clubface lightly with the knuckle of the index finger on your opposite hand. When you find the spot on the face where the clubhead rebounds straight backward instead of twisting, you've located the sweet spot. That's the point on the clubface that you want to make contact with; you may want to mark the top of the putterhead so you'll have a clear indication of where it is when you address the ball.

Your putter may have already been marked, courtesy of the

manufacturer, but it's still a good idea to check for the exact location, since the existing mark may not be accurate.

To enhance the chances of solid contact, mark the ball and adjust it so the trademark is lined up directly with the target line but turned back toward the putterface, so that when you set the clubhead behind the ball at address, the trademark and the sweet-spot mark are adjacent to each other. When you make the stroke, concentrate on striking the trademark with the sweet-spot mark on the putter.

If mishitting putts has been a problem for you, making solid contact on a regular basis will be a big lift to your putting game. Not only will you get the ball to the hole more, but you'll also get more satisfaction out of the feeling of hitting the ball solidly.

THINK "DISTANCE"

Every so often you'll leave a putt short and think to yourself, "I forgot to hit it." Or, you work hard to determine the line of a big-breaking putt, then step up to it and hit the ball way too hard, blasting it through the break so it never has a chance. This kind of thing happens a lot—the golfer becomes so preoccupied with determining the line of the putt that he forgets to devote enough concentration to the distance. If you've got a putt that you consider makable, remember that determining the line is only half the job—you've got to think about the distance and how hard you must hit it to make it go that far.

PUTTING PSYCHOLOGY

Putting doesn't take much physical effort—think about the difference between cracking a good drive and rolling a ball ten feet. The ability to putt well has more to do with psychology than anything else.

Most players judge their putting skill by how consistent they are in the short range—ten feet or less. Any player who misses a lot of short putts will not consider himself a good putter, and the constant blows to the psyche that come from missing a lot of short putts are hard on morale. A popular saying notes that "golf is a game of inches," but putting actually comes down to fractions of inches—often the difference between making a putt and lipping out. Having to tap in a ball that hangs on the lip counts the same as a tee shot ripped 270 yards down the middle of the fairway: One stroke.

One of the worst things that can happen to a golfer is losing confidence in the ability to sink a short putt in the three-to-five-foot range. What makes a short putt so mentally demanding is that it's a shot that you are expected to convert. You can miss a 15-foot putt and, although you wish you'd made it, you won't feel too bad about it because trying to hit a 4.25-inch target from that far away isn't the easiest thing to do. But once you get within about five feet from the hole, you expect to make it. You feel that it's a needless waste of a stroke if the ball doesn't go in. And it is. But the fact is, everybody misses a short putt now and then. There have been a number of short putts missed on the final holes of tournaments that have cost the player who struck it either an outright win or a chance to tie. In the 1979 Masters, Ed Sneed left a four-footer on the eighteenth hole hanging on the lip; had it dropped, he would have been the winner. Instead, it put him into a playoff with Tom Watson and Fuzzy Zoeller; Zoeller claimed it with a birdie on the second playoff hole. One year earlier, Hubie Green had let a similar putt slide by the edge on 18 at Augusta; he finished a shot behind Gary Player. In the 1947 U.S. Open, Sam Snead and Lew Worsham tied for first after the regulation four rounds, then reached the final green of the eighteen-hole playoff still tied. Each faced a putt of less than three feet for a score of 69 that would send them out for another eighteen. Worsham called for a measurement, and it was found that Snead was away; he putted and missed for a 70, while Worsham followed by sinking his for a 69 and the trophy.

These stories aren't meant to scare you, but rather to show that even the best players in the world are capable of missing a short putt. Everyone is. If you suddenly find yourself having a problem sinking short putts consistently, you need to get your confidence back fast. Otherwise, it will put pressure on the rest of your putting game to leave a very short tap-in every time. Following are some tips to regain your short putting ability.

Change Your Grip

A simple change in the way you hold the putter can give your stroke a fresh feeling, which may be all you need to get back on track. Changing your grip is often a good antidote for all kinds of putting blahs, not just from short distances. Ian Baker-Finch, an excellent putter, regularly changes the way he holds the putter by extending one or both index fingers, or not extending either, depending on what feels best. He may change from day to day, or even mid-round.

Don't be afraid to experiment with how you place your fingers on the club. As long as your grip gives you a secure hold while allowing freedom of motion and good feedback, it can't be wrong.

Ram the Ball Home

The more you miss putts, the less positive you'll be from a mental standpoint and the more tentative your stroke will become. Nothing destroys a true forwardswing path like decelerating the clubhead, so if you've been trying to topple the short ones in, only to see them slide by the edge, change your attack and start ramming them into the back of the cup. Exaggerate your follow-through and keep the clubface moving straight down the target line toward the cup.

Shorten Your Backswing

Another cure for deceleration is to swing the putterhead back only half as far as you normally would. By limiting how far you take the club back, you'll be forced to accelerate through in order to get the ball to the hole.

Start Short—*Really* Short

Practice putting from very short range—no more than one foot away. Stroke twenty balls. Increase the distance to a foot and a half. Stroke twenty more balls. Keep increasing the distance by six inches, each time hitting twenty balls, until you're hitting four-footers. Keep track of how many putts you've made from each location. If you make less than fifteen from a particular distance, retreat six inches and start over again from there.

Shrink the Target

Instead of putting to a cup, plant a tee in the practice green and try to roll the ball into it from five feet away. If you do this for a half-hour, an actual cup will appear the size of a pothole, and getting the ball into it will seem a lot easier.

Keep Your Hands and Putterhead in a Dead Heat

The less confidence you have, the more nervous you're likely to be, and nervousness causes physical tension that can disrupt your ability to make a smooth stroke. And a jerky stroke is likely to result in a poor swing path. To avoid these problems, concentrate on keeping your hands and the putterhead moving at the same pace, so neither gets ahead of the other. Imagine that they are in a neck-and-neck race on the backswing and forwardswing, and that both arrive at the ball at the same time. Keep them moving in a dead heat until well after the ball has been struck. You'll find that doing this will force you to make an even, un-hurried, pendulum-like motion, resulting in solid contact and a putt that rolls on the intended line.

Watch a Spot

Head movement is an easy trap to fall into because the target is so close on short putts that it's natural to want to look up quickly to see whether the putt has dropped or not. Problems occur, though, when you move to look before the ball has been struck. Even if it's only a split-second before impact, excess head move-ment will make your body move, throwing off the path of the clubhead and misdirecting the putt. The worst part of this error is that when you start missing putts, anxiety sets in, so you tend to start looking up even quicker—and a vicious cycle begins. To put a stop to it, you need to focus on something that will keep your head and body still through impact.

One way is to focus of a spot on the ground directly in front of the ball and keep your attention there until after the putter-head passes over it of the forwardswing. If you can do that, you will have successfully kept your body still. This is a trick that Payne Stewart has been known to use.

Another way is to concentrate on keeping your eyes focused down on the ground and, instead of looking to see if the ball has

To help keep your head and body still when putting, focus your attention on a spot directly in front of the ball and keep your eye there until after the putterhead has passed it on the forwardswing.

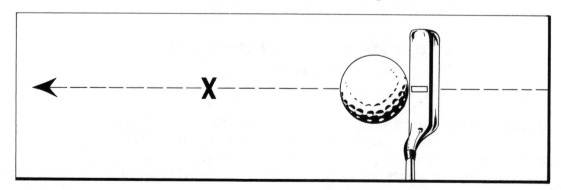

When you're in a slump, continue to visualize positive results, and things will eventually turn around.

gone in, *listening* for it to drop. This is a favorite method of Gary Player, who has sunk his share of short putts.

A final way to keep your head and body still is to keep your head down and not look to see where the ball is going until after the putterhead has swung past your left ear.

DON'T LOSE HEART IN A SLUMP

Every golfer suffers a putting slump from time to time. It's not uncommon to hear a pro lament that he was hitting the ball well from tee to green, but just couldn't get the putts to drop. The worst thing that you can do in these situations is to allow yourself to get too worried about the current circumstances. Remain confident, continue to visualize positive results, and take steps to troubleshoot your stroke.

Eventually, you'll right the problem and your putting will turn around.

TROUBLE
PLAY

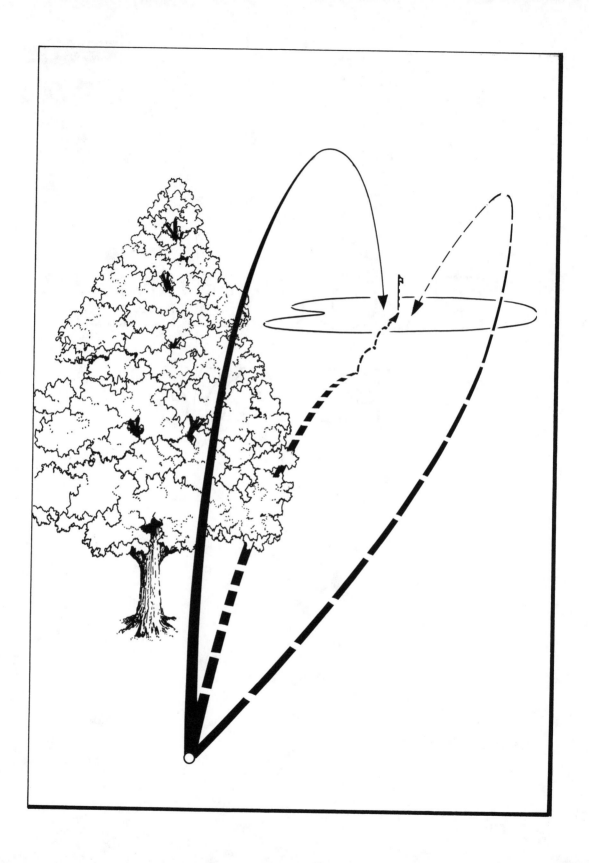

OFF THE FAIRWAY

When you get into trouble, the need to focus closely on the shot at hand is even more important than usual, since the lie is working against you, making solid contact difficult. To have the most success on trouble shots, you have to understand how the situation will affect your ability to strike the ball cleanly, and then make whatever adjustments are necessary to maximize the chances of making good contact and hitting an acceptable shot. When your ball ends up in a position of particularly difficult trouble, don't abandon your normal mental preparation routine and quickly flail away. When the going gets rough, you'll need to pause and use your mental abilities to focus your concentration and plan the best possible way to get out of an extraordinary situation. Not that you'll always be successful, but the odds are that you'll hit a better shot than if you take a quick, disgusted thrash. And whether you hit a particularly good shot or not, you'll feel better mentally that you took the time to think it out and put forth your best effort.

ROUGH

The most common hazard you're likely to run into is rough, which is the high grass that usually borders fairways and sometimes surrounds the green. Rough is a penalty for hitting an inaccurate shot, the height of the grass making it harder to get the clubface cleanly on the ball than if it were on the short grass of the fairway. Often it exists in varying degrees. If so, the *first cut* of rough is what borders the fairway, the penalty for a slightly errant shot. A wilder shot will find the *second cut*, which is higher and thus more difficult to negotiate than the first. There may also be a *third cut*, which offers stiff punishment for those who stray far from the beaten path.

How much of a problem rough presents depends on the characteristics of the grass. The taller, thicker, greener and healthier the blades are, the more resistance they will put on the clubhead as you swing it down toward the ball. A patch of rough that is relatively short, sparse and brittle will offer a lot less resistance than rough that is tall, lush and abundant. If the blades are growing away from you, the clubhead will slide through much easier than if they are growing toward you.

The type of lie that you get will also determine how difficult the shot will be. If the ball is sitting "down," it means that it has settled downward in the grass, making it tougher to get the clubface onto it. If the ball is sitting "up," it's resting on top of the rough on a cushion of grass. This will make it easier to get the clubface on the ball, but doesn't necessarily mean it will be an easy shot, since it's possible to swing the clubhead too far underneath the ball and pop it up. (The best way to handle this situation is to imagine the ball is on a tee and try to pick it off cleanly.

How good you are at playing out of the rough will depend a great deal on how well you can judge the limitations it puts on your club selection. As mentioned earlier, the problem that rough poses is that it gets in the way of the clubhead as it approaches the ball, slowing it down and perhaps twisting it open or closed before contact. How much the rough will interfere with club-to-ball contact depends on its characteristics. For the most part, it's best to avoid trying to hit long irons out of even light rough, because the shallow downswing path is likely to slow the clubhead and turn the clubface open or closed. If you need distance, a better option is a 4- or 5-wood, since their rounded heads and broad flat soles tend to slide cleanly through high grass instead of getting bogged down in it.

However, if the severity of the situation won't allow a fairway wood, you'll have to back down to a shorter iron and accept less distance. Remember, the steeper the downswing, the less grass the clubhead will have to fight through to get to the ball, and thus the better your chances of getting the ball safely out. Don't make the mistake of trying to force the ball out of the rough with too much club at the risk of moving it only a few feet. That's why at the U.S. Open, where the rough is traditionally very severe in order to help create a stern test of golf, you'll often see players ignore the green and opt to hit a pitching wedge from the rough back to the fairway. They realize they won't be able to get at the ball with anything other than the steep swing and sharp leading edge of a wedge.

Of course, the club you are able to use to get out of the rough will depend on your physical strength. Players with strong hands who build a lot of clubhead speed will be able to power the clubhead through high grass with more success than players with less strength. An example of this occurred at the 1961 British Open at Royal Birkdale. Arnold Palmer was leading the tournament in the final round when he reached the 15th tee, trying to hold off a charge by Dai Rees, a Welshman. Hitting into a strong left-to-right wind on the par four, Palmer let his tee shot get away to the right, where it landed in heavy rough. From there he debated between wedging safely back to the fairway and trying to pitch on and one-putt for par, or trying to tear it out with a 6-iron in an attempt to reach the green. Realizing that Rees was close behind and gaining, Palmer opted for the 6-iron and went after the ball with all the power he could muster. He tore a divot almost a foot long out of the rough, but when the dust cleared, the ball was resting on the green. From there he two-putted for par and went on to win by a single stroke over Rees. Few golfers would have had the physical ability to do what Palmer did, but if you've got the strength, you'll be able to get the ball out of the rough more effectively than the average player.

Watch for Fliers

Even if you do happen to draw a decent lie in the rough, you'll have a harder time than usual controlling the ball because you won't be able to put any backspin on it. Thus, the ensuing shot will be a "flier" that flies lower and farther than usual, and rolls more upon landing. Plan for it by taking less club, aiming to land the ball short of the target and bouncing it up.

HARDPAN

Another kind of trouble you may find off the fairway, especially during the hot summer months, is what's known as hardpan—a grassless patch of ground that's been baked very hard by the sun. Most golf courses won't waste water on anything other than fairways, tees and greens during the height of summer, so areas of hardpan may appear here and there off the fairway. Playing a shot from hardpan is a lot like hitting off a concrete surface. You've got to guard against hitting behind the ball, because then the clubhead will skip off the ground and the leading edge of the clubface will strike the ball's midsection, "bellying" it on a very low, hard line. There are two ways to play off hardpan. The first is best suited for hitting from the 6-iron to fairway woods: Address the ball normally but shade your weight back toward your heels slightly. The idea is to sweep the ball away cleanly. Take care, however, not to put too much weight on your heels, or you'll risk rocking backward and topping the ball.

The second way to play from hardpan, best suited for the 7-iron to sand wedge, is to move the ball back in your stance and "trap" it against the ground, decreasing your chances of mishitting it. To play the shot this way, set up slightly open, with the ball just behind center and your left hand just ahead of the ball. Because you're trapping the ball, you've got to prevent the toe from passing the heel through impact as it normally would, or you'll end up smothering the ball into the ground. In order to keep the right hand from rolling over the left and closing the clubface, keep your left hand and wrist firm through the hitting zone. The shot will fly lower than usual and bend from left to right. It will also have a great deal of bite: If you land it on the green, it will take one bounce and then hold fast.

When you have to play a short shot off hardpan onto the green, it's usually best to play the ball back in your stance and try to bump it short and roll it to the target with a low-lofted club instead of trying to hit it high with a wedge, because, once again, your chances of mishitting the ball and getting a poor result will be decreased.

FAIRWAY SAND

Another problem you can run into if you miss the fairway is sand. As when playing from hardpan, the foremost thing to avoid from this hazard is hitting behind the ball. Although you intentionally hit behind the ball when exploding from a greenside trap, that kind of shot is limited in the distance you can hit it. Long explosions rarely travel more than 50 yards, because sand acts as a buffer when it comes between the club and the ball, deadening impact and preventing the ball from springing powerfully off the face. That's why the explosion is not favorable from fairway sand, when you will usually want to hit the ball much longer. To get the kind of distance you need, you'll have to make contact with the ball before the sand.

To hit the shot, play the ball about half a ball-width farther back than usual to enhance the chances of hitting the ball first. Dig your feet into the sand slightly and then angle the soles of your feet outward a little for stability. Take a little bit of the flex out of your knees and hover the clubhead behind the ball (grounding the club in a fairway bunker is a two-shot penalty). Concentrate on keeping the angle of your spine constant while making a three-quarter swing—no more—for the sake of club-head control. You may not get the ball on the green, but at the very least you'll get it out of the bunker. The last thing you want is to mishit the ball and leave it in there.

The club you choose should depend on the lie and whether the bunker has a lip that you have to hit over. It's possible to hit a 3-wood from fairway sand if the lie is clean and the lip is low. But when deciding how much loft you'll need to clear the lip, remember that you're playing the ball back in your stance, so the ball will fly lower than usual, and also that you're only making a three-quarter swing, so the ball won't rise as quickly as usual.

Another type of fairway sand that's becoming more and more a part of modern golf course design is known as a "waste bunker." This is typically a vast, flat patch of hard, coarse sand that guards tee-shot landing areas. The same technique for getting out of fairway bunkers will work, but you are allowed to ground your club behind the ball at address from a waste bunker without penalty.

OUT OF THE WOODS

Hitting the ball into trees from time to time is a fact of golfing life. So, then, is getting out of them. To do that you need to know how to hit the ball high and low, and how to bend it left and right to get the shot to the target despite the obstacle. Refer back to chapter 8 on shotmaking for help with these shots. But there are a few other tricks you ought to have in your bag to help get out of the woods safely.

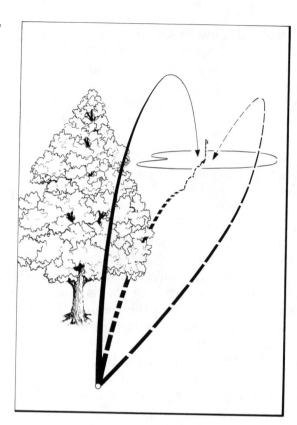

When playing from the woods, always consider all options— going over, under or around.

Consider All Options

Take time to visualize all the options when trying to get out of the woods. Is the best route to go over, under or around? Don't forget that if you're deep in the trees, you should always look up to see if there's some kind of opening up high that you may be able to get the ball through. This is definitely a tricky stunt to try to pull off, but it could be the exit you need if you're really in a bind.

Don't Forget the Driver

An excellent club to use to keep the ball low under branches is the driver, because it will naturally keep the ball down without your having to make any adjustments in ball position. You should be able to swing hard and still not worry about the ball rising too high as long as you sweep the ball cleanly off the ground instead of hitting down with a descending blow and popping the ball up.

Threading a Needle

When playing out of trees, you may be faced with having to hit the ball through a narrow gap formed by tree trunks. This requires accuracy. If you're only trying to get back to the fairway, don't try to press the ball through a narrow opening unless you really feel it's worth the risk. It's better to play safe when you can, because if you happen to hit a tree, the ball could ricochet even deeper into trouble, and before you know it, you've made triple bogey.

To increase your chances of hitting the ball though a narrow gap, keep the ball as low as possible, since it's easier to hit a low shot on a straight line than a high shot. Pick out an intermediate target to help make sure that your aim is precise—if you're off by just a little, you could bounce the ball off trees. Lastly, relax your arms and make a smooth swing, striving for solid contact. The biggest mistake amateurs make when trying to hit this kind of shot is tensing up, which causes a poor downswing path so they either push or pull the ball off line and get a negative result. Trust that you've aimed well, keep your head down, make a smooth, rhythmic swing, and the ball will shoot through the gap and safely out of the woods.

HILLY LIES

Finding the fairway doesn't guarantee that you'll have a great lie. If your ball isn't on level ground, it will be more difficult to make solid contact and get the ball to the target. To play your level best from sloping ground, you need to make certain adjustments in your setup to better the chances of getting the clubface squarely on the ball. Remember, though, that the adjustments you make and the effects of the particular type of slope you're playing from will affect the shape and trajectory of the shot. Understanding and planning for these effects is crucial to making a successful swing.

Before addressing how to play from unlevel lies, it's worth noting that it's best to avoid them when you can, since anything that adds to the difficulty of hitting and aiming the ball will make it harder to score well. Therefore, when planning a tee shot or lay-up on a par five, pick out a landing area that will offer you the best combination of a level lie and a decent angle to the green. If using a driver will result in hitting your approach from a downhill lie, consider laying up with less club off the tee, since hitting a 150-yard approach from flat ground is easier than from 135 yards off a severe downslope.

You won't always be able to avoid sloping lies, however, so it's not a bad idea to devote a little practice time to learning how to play them. Most players who are thrown off when they find their ball on a hill are the ones who hit all of their practice balls off perfectly level ground. The next time you are out on the course by yourself, make it a point to practice some shots from uphill, downhill and sidehill lies.

DOWNHILL

When the ball is on a downslope, so your left foot is lower than your right foot, you need to play the ball farther back in the center of your stance to increase the chances of making solid contact and decrease the chances of hitting behind the ball. Let the degree of slope be your guide: If the grade is steep, move it back to the center of your stance; if it's only a slight downslope, moving it just a fraction back will suffice.

At address, gravity will force your weight more toward your left foot, so keep your left knee braced and firm so your hips and shoulders are approximately parallel to the angle of the ground. How much weight is on the left foot will depend on how steep the hill is.

Make a low, long takeaway, so the clubhead follows the line of the ground, and try to duplicate that arc on the downswing path. Doing the opposite—picking up the club abruptly—increases your chances of chopping down into the ground behind

Make sure that your body lines are parallel to the slope when playing from a downhill or uphill lie.

the ball. Take one less club than you would normally need, since the angle of the slope will decrease the effective loft of the clubface, making the shot fly lower and longer. Because of this, the most difficult clubs to hit from a downhill lie are those with the least loft, fairway woods and long irons—a factor to consider when deciding what to hit.

Because the angle of the slope is going to force your lower body toward the target more abruptly than from a level lie, it will be tougher to stay behind the ball with your upper body and release the club through impact. The result will be a shot that bends from left to right.

UPHILL

Contrary to playing off a downhill lie, an upslope will force your weight toward your right side; this time make sure your right knee remains braced and the weight stays firmly on the inside of your right foot. This is especially important on the backswing, when it's easy to make the mistake of letting your body sway onto the outside of your foot.

For the most part, it's easier to make good contact from an uphill lie than from a downhill lie, provided you set your body lines parallel to the slope and make the same effort to perform a low takeaway so the clubhead follows the angle of the slope the first few feet it moves away from the ball. Picking it up abruptly

Take the clubhead back low so it follows the line of the slope when playing from an uphill or downhill lie.

will lead to chopping down and popping the ball up.

The upslope will add to the effective loft of the club, making the shot fly higher and shorter than normal, so take more club than you think you'll need. In the 1991 Players Championship, Fuzzy Zoeller drove errantly on number 14 in the third round, a short par four. His ball rested only 120 yards from the green—about 9-iron distance—but was on a severe upslope. From a very awkward stance, Fuzz hit a 5-iron that shot nearly straight in the air, hung for what seemed forever, then dropped nearly straight from the sky and landed a foot and a half from the hole.

Because the upslope will cause your upper body to stay well behind the ball through impact, promoting a quicker release of the hands, the shot will bend from right to left.

BALL BELOW THE FEET

Whenever the ball is on a sideslope, you again have to make adjustments in your address position in order to counteract the effects of the slope and better your chances of hitting the ball solidly. As a rule, you should rest the clubhead on the ground behind the ball so the sole is flat against the slope, and then position your body in relation to the club. The angle of the hill will force your weight forward, but don't let it slide past the balls of your feet to your toes, or else you may lose your balance going forward on the downswing, causing a heeled or shanked shot.

When the ball is below the feet, you'll be forced to compensate by bending more at the waist and standing closer to it than usual. This will cause you to swing on an upright swing plane, producing a left-to-right shot. The degree of bend will correspond to the degree of slope so that a severe slope will cause a severe bend in the shot.

The tendency in this situation is to top the shot because the ball is below your normal hitting zone. Guard against this by concentrating on maintaining the angle of your spine on the downswing instead of lifting it through impact. Generally, it's easier for the average player to make contact with the lower clubs from this kind of lie because their longer shafts don't require them to bend as much. However, the straighter faces of the lower clubs will also impart more sidespin on the ball, making it curve more. So although it will be easier to make contact with a 3-iron when the ball is below the feet, the shot will curve more than if you used a higher club like a 7-iron.

BALL ABOVE THE FEET

If the ground slopes so that the ball is positioned above your feet, you should again rest the clubhead behind the ball so the sole is flat to the ground, and then position your body in relation to the club. The nature of the slope will force you to stand farther away from the ball and straighter at the knees and waist, resulting in a flatter than normal swing plane that will produce a right-to-left shot. How much depends on the severity of the slope and the specific club you choose.

The most common mistake when playing from this type of lie is to hit behind the ball; again, key on keeping your spine angle constant and try to sweep the ball off the ground to combat that kind of mishit.

WIND

Wind is the invisible force that can turn an easy course into a difficult one, and a difficult course into a colossal test of skill and patience. Seaside courses are usually constructed with the prevailing wind in mind as a constant force to be negotiated and dealt with, like rough and sand. Hence the old Scottish saying, "If there's na'wind, there's na' go'f." Most tour players will agree that a golf course is at its most defenseless when conditions are calm, because then they don't have to contend with any forces beating the ball back, ballooning it past the intended mark or pushing it right or left. Matters of club selection and aiming the ball at the target become much simpler. Such windless conditions are rare, however, so it's important for every golfer to learn how to deal with a breeze.

The wind can be a help or a hindrance, depending on its strength and direction; it can have a great effect on the shot being played or little at all. But one thing about the wind is that you can't change it; if it blows, it blows. What you can do, though, is alter the shape of your shots so they will be less affected, and avoid certain shot shapes that are more likely to be influenced by the wind.

HEADWINDS

The average golfer probably worries more about a headwind than any other because he knows it's going to cost him distance, something most handicap players can ill afford to lose. Not only will a headwind hold the ball back, it will also increase its backspin, making it fly higher and shorter.

The usual response is to try to swing harder when the wind is in your face. This is a mistake because a headwind will usually compound most impact errors. It will increase backspin or left-to-right spin, so a skied shot will fly even higher and shorter, while a fade or slice will sail even farther to the right. So right away, you've got to adjust your attitude and accept the fact that you may lose some distance, and that trying to swing harder is going to cause more problems than it's worth. Instead, make it your top priority to get the clubface squarely on the ball instead of trying to build some extra clubhead speed.

The second biggest mistake the average player makes when playing directly into the wind is underestimating how much distance he will lose. When hitting an approach shot, you don't need to swing harder, but instead should simply take more club. Yet most casual players are chronically short into the wind because they fail to take enough stick. A good rule of thumb is to go up one club for approximately every ten miles-per-hour of wind. So if you normally hit a 7-iron from 150 yards out under calm conditions, and the wind is blowing 20 mph in your face, you need to move up to a 5-iron. Typically, amateurs feel uncomfortable going up or down more than one club, but you definitely need to make big adjustments if the wind is very strong. (Of course you won't be able to tell exactly how fast the wind is blowing when you're on the course, but experience will help you determine what club to choose. The point here is, don't be shy about taking a lot more club if the wind is heavy—rarely will you come up short of the target when it is.)

Because wind moves faster at high altitudes, the best play into a headwind off the tee is a low draw that bores through the air under the stronger current above and runs well after landing. On approach shots, you can do two things, depending on the strength of the wind. If it is moderate, you may want to take more club and use the wind to hit a higher, soft-landing shot into the green. However, if you're hitting into the teeth of a stiff breeze you may want to play a low "knockdown" shot and bump the ball to your target instead of trying to carry it there.

Hitting directly into the wind can also help you on certain

short shots, such as pitches and explosions shots, making them fly up higher and land steeper so they stop more quickly.

Wind
169

TAILWINDS

A tailwind is usually considered favorable because it carries the ball farther, adding distance. It also tends to minimize sidespin, helping straighten out a potentially crooked shot. The negative aspect of a wind at your back so that it also reduces backspin, flattening out the trajectory so the ball flies lower and lands on a shallow line, bouncing sharply forward instead of stopping quickly. This makes it difficult to calculate distance control when driving to tight landing areas and hitting approach shots. Always take a careful look at what lies behind your target and visualize the possibilities if the ball should happen to go long.

Although knockdown shots are normally played into the wind, you may want to consider playing a low shot under a tailwind if it is extremely strong and you are in a situation where you are short-iron distance from your target.

CROSSWINDS

There are two ways to deal with a crosswind. If it is moderate but strong enough to have an effect on the flight of the ball, you can "ride" the wind by aiming away from the target and shaping the shot so it bends in the same direction. This way the wind carries the ball slightly in the direction it is blowing. The other way is to hit a "hold" shot by bending the ball into the wind so the lateral movement is canceled out and the shot flies relatively straight.

If a crosswind is very strong, you'll be forced to ride it, but you should still work the ball against it if you can to minimize the degree the shot will be blown off course. Again, the lower the shot, the less it will be bothered by the wind, so low, boring long irons will be less affected than high-flying fairway woods and short irons, and knockdown shots may be appropriate.

When riding the wind, don't haphazardly aim away from the target. During your preshot routine make it a point to pick out a secondary target on whichever side of the green you're aiming. Visualize the shot starting out toward it, then floating on the wind toward your primary target and landing there.

Heavy crosswinds will make it much more difficult to get the ball to the target. One of your priorities when playing in this kind of condition is not only to allow for the wind when aiming, but also to guard against aiming near hazards if there is a chance that the ball could get blown into trouble. It requires a lot of thought and patience to score well on a hole when the wind is blowing sideways, and you should worry less about hitting small targets and simply be satisfied to put the ball in the fairway and on the green.

MISCELLANEOUS TROUBLE

There are a few other trouble situations that may come up occasionally. Although you may not run into them as often as those previously mentioned, you should still know how to play them just in case.

HEAVY GREENSIDE ROUGH

Sometimes you'll play a course where the superintendent has allowed the grass around the greens to grow into very heavy rough. If you miss the green and your ball ends up buried in this kind of stuff, you're in for a difficult and unpredictable shot. If you try to drop the clubhead straight down on the ball, it may either get caught up in the grass, moving the ball only a fraction of the distance intended, or the club may slice cleanly through the grass so the ball flies out fast and goes too far.

A better way to get out of this kind of lie is to play it in the same manner you explode from sand. With a sand wedge, open your stance and the blade, cock your wrists quickly and hit about one inch behind the ball. Your swing should be long and smooth, not short and quick, and, most important, follow through so the clubhead clears the grass. If the club gets caught and stalls in the rough, the ball will hardly move. You'll see this

To play out of heavy greenside rough, hit behind the ball and "explode" it as if from sand.

type of shot played often in the U.S. Open, when the rough is typically very high around the greens.

Take a second to visualize what actually happens at impact when exploding from rough: The clubhead strikes down behind the ball, creating a cushion of grass between the ball and clubface. If you keep the clubhead moving, the force will drive the ball out on a high, soft trajectory. You'll have to swing harder than usual to hit the shot the desired distance in order to make up for the resistance and cushioning effect of the grass behind the ball, so the most common mistake is for the player to lose his nerve and decelerate on the downswing. This is certain to cause you to leave the ball in the rough. Make sure to swing briskly through, so you at least get the ball onto the green, and remember that even tour pros consider themselves somewhat lucky when they put this kind of shot close. Knowing how to deal with this situation is extremely valuable, so take some practice time to get familiar with it if you aren't already.

WATER

Ninety-nine percent of the time you hit into water, you're going to have to take a one-shot penalty, and sometimes distance, depending on whether the hazard was lateral or not. The other one percent of the time you may have a playable shot, but even then you should seriously consider if it's worth the risk. Only try to play the ball out of water if at least half the ball is above the water and you can assume a stable, balanced address position. If neither of these conditions is in your favor, your odds of getting the ball out are very slim, and there's nothing worse than hitting an unsuccessful shot from water. Besides wasting a shot and leaving the ball in the drink, you'll also no doubt get soaked!

But hitting out of water can be done and may be worth it if you pull it off. To play the shot, take a pitching wedge, position the ball in the center of your stance with your hands ahead of the ball. That way the clubface is angled and can slice straight down into the water and under the ball. Hover the clubhead above the surface (touching the water with the clubhead at address is a two-shot penalty), pick it up very sharply with a quick cock of the wrists and hit down hard about two inches behind the ball. The idea is the same as when exploding from sand in that you want to explode the water surrounding the ball out of the hazard, taking the ball with it, so be sure to keep the club moving and follow through clear of the water. It may help to visualize the club moving a small wall of water out of the hazard.

If you decide to play a ball out of water, make up your mind to give it your best shot. It's easy to "chicken out" on the downswing and flinch or decelerate, since you're probably going to get a face full of water! With that in mind, you may as well stay with the shot through impact, since you're going to get wet anyway.

RICOCHET SHOTS

If your ball ever comes to rest in a position where an object behind it obstructs your ability to make much of a backswing, you have two options. One is to play the ball laterally (not directly at your target) simply to get it away from the obstruction. The other way is to turn around and try to ricochet the ball off the impeding obstacle and back toward your target. This kind of play is best made at greenside, but it may also be a good option if you've driven next to a tree in the woods and you just want to get back to the fairway.

Tom Watson played a ricochet shot in the final round of the 1984 British Open at St. Andrews. Trailing Seve Ballesteros by a shot, Watson overshot the green of the long par-four 17th, known as the Road Hole. His ball came to rest close by a stone wall that crosses behind the green, sharply restricting his backswing. Watson's response was to punch the ball directly into the wall so it caromed back and onto the putting surface, where he two-putted for a bogey five. (Ballesteros, however, playing in the group ahead, finished with a birdie on eighteen to win by two strokes over Watson and Bernhard Langer.)

If you think the situation is right for a ricochet shot, take care to judge both the surface you'll be glancing the ball off and the angle that you'll be hitting the ball on so that it doesn't bounce back and hit you. Not only could this result in injury, but it's also a two-stroke penalty if you are struck, even if only slightly, by your own shot. Use a club with enough loft to get the ball up so it doesn't ricochet straight back and hit the club face—that will also cost you two penalty strokes. Also, because the direction of the shot may be unpredictable, be careful that you don't ricochet into more trouble.

About the Author

Kenneth Van Kampen spent four years as an associate editor for *Golf Magazine*, where he wrote numerous instruction articles, many with tour players such as Payne Stewart, Fred Couples, Paul Azinger and Raymond Floyd. He has also coauthored two instruction books, *Play Great Golf* with Arnold Palmer and *Win and Win Again* with Curtis Strange. Originally from Albany, New York, Van Kampen graduated from St. Michael's College and currently resides in Manhattan.